Arizona Estate Administration

Answer Book

Arizona Estate Administration Answer Book

**Practical Answers to Common Questions
For Any Size Estate in Arizona**

Thomas J. Bouman

Attorney at Law

**Published by Lulu, Inc.
Raleigh, NC**

Arizona Estate Administration Answer Book

Published by:

Lulu, Inc.
3101 Hillsborough St.
Raleigh, NC 27607-5436

In association with:

Thomas J. Bouman, PLLC
7650 E. Broadway Blvd. #108
Tucson, AZ 85710

Thomas J. Bouman, PLLC is an Arizona limited liability company, doing business as Bouman Law Firm. Its sole principal, Thomas J. Bouman, is a member in good standing of the State Bar of Arizona.

ISBN 978-1-365-22190-3

This intent of this publication is to provide accurate information concerning the subject matter covered; however, any project of this nature will have errors and omissions. Please direct comments, suggestions, or corrections by mail to the author for inclusion in later editions.

This publication is not intended to substitute for the advice of an attorney. If you require legal or other expert advice, you should seek the services of a competent attorney or other professional.

TABLE OF CONTENTS

This book is intended to provide general information regarding the laws applicable to the administration of an estate, and to provide suggestions regarding appropriate actions for different situations. It is not intended as a substitute for the reader's own research, or for the advice of a qualified estate administration specialist. The author and publisher shall have neither liability nor responsibility to any person or entity with respect to any loss or damage caused, or alleged to be caused, directly or indirectly by the information contained in this book.

ARS citations refer to the Arizona Revised Statutes in effect as of publication. For a copy of the actual statute, visit your local law library or the following website:

http://www.azleg.gov/ArizonaRevisedStatutes.asp

Introduction

The purpose of this book is to address practical issues that commonly arise upon the death of an Arizona resident or a non-Arizona resident who owned property in Arizona. Although a substantial amount of general information is provided regarding estate administration, this book emphasizes the unique aspects of Arizona law whenever possible.

Estate administration is by its nature a sobering topic of study. An appreciation of the brevity of life and the futility of attempting to control the uncontrollable are prerequisites for all who approach it. However, the task of preparing for the inevitable by making informed decisions is certainly cathartic and often liberating to a large extent. It can provide release from the heavy burdens of worry and uncertainty for both a dying person and that person's loved ones.

What is an estate?

The term "estate" refers to a deceased person's property and assets of all types. The property a person owns at the time of death, combined with any additional assets made available as a result of death, are together referred to as the deceased person's estate. A living person has property and assets while a deceased person has an estate. The term also may refer to debts and liabilities of the deceased person. Of course, a creditor will seek payment in full whether the debtor is alive or not.

What is estate administration?

The term "estate administration" refers to the closing of a deceased person's financial affairs and property interests. In some cases the process of estate administration may be simple to complete, but it can also be overwhelming in scope and complexity. Many estates will require a probate action, some require a trust termination, and others will require both. However, many estates can be administered without any formal action at all. They might rely on the effect of property titling rules, beneficiary designations, and small estate affidavits. The term estate administration is used broadly to cover all of these possible situations.

The typical tasks required during estate administration include:

- Make final arrangements for the body
- Protect and secure important property
- Determine whether probate or trustee appointment is needed
- Identify the heirs and beneficiaries
- Pay debts, expenses, and claims
- Determine the appropriate methods for distribution of assets

What are the basic components of an estate plan?

In Arizona, the following documents are commonly used for estate planning purposes:

- *Last will and testament.* The will designates someone to administer the estate and clarifies who should receive any property that must be distributed by probate action.
- *General durable power of attorney.* This document designates someone to manage the financial affairs of its signer in the event of the signer's extended mental incapacity.
- *Health care power of attorney.* This document designates someone to make decisions regarding the signer's health care should the signer be unable to communicate.
- *Living will declaration.* This document provides instructions and guidelines to the health care agent regarding end-of-life decisions.
- *HIPAA release.* This document gives consent for the release of protected health care information to designated persons.

For those with more advanced needs, an estate plan might include a revocable living trust, business entity, or irrevocable trust.

Estate planning also refers to how property and accounts are titled, including beneficiary designations. For those who fail to make formal plans, Arizona law provides a statutory estate plan with rigid, default rules for distribution of assets.

Why is estate administration so difficult?

Any person who agrees to administer an estate takes on enormous responsibility. The project is rarely simple and usually goes without a hint of gratitude from others. Most administrators work without pay even though it can add hundreds of hours of work to their busy schedules.

Estate administration is challenging because no two estates are the same. We all have our own jigsaw puzzle of assets, which can change at any time. Add to that the reality that no two families are the same. Mix in the possibility of a second marriage, pending divorce, disabled child, poor money management, foreign assets, timeshare ownership, businesses, creditor issues, black sheep children, family loans, etc. – you get the idea – and even the smallest estate can have some very large problems to deal with. No matter how much we might dislike politicians and attorneys, they do act on behalf of real people with varying beliefs and expectations. The laws we have reflect the interests of our people. Unfortunately, the laws often struggle to bridge the gap between uniformity and freedom of choice. But as confusing as the laws are, the prudent administrator will have the best chance of success by starting with the most important step.

What is the most important step in estate administration?

Never underestimate the importance of getting the facts right at the beginning. Do not rely on what you believe to be true, or what others tell you they believe to be true. If you are responsible for administering an estate, your mission must be to get an accurate understanding of what the deceased person owned and owed. Trouble and frustration pursue the administrator who rushes this task. You need primary source information: bank statements, real estate deeds, beneficiary designations, tax returns. Without primary source information, you are driving at night without headlights. Get the facts right, and then proceed cautiously.

What are some basic principles to follow?

Start by keeping a realistic perspective, then:

- Be patient.
- Get the facts.
- Be scrupulously honest and let others verify it.
- Make informed decisions and be decisive about them.
- Accept the first reasonable offer when listing a property for sale. The second offer is rarely as good.
- Take the time to listen to disgruntled heirs. They will usually feel better because of it, even when they don't get what they want.
- Keep track of all receipts and expenses from day one.
- Never trust the *legal* counsel of someone working at a bank or credit union; or insurance agency or title company for that matter.
- Always give timely notice to heirs and beneficiaries.
- When in doubt, change the locks.

What is the best way to read this book?

Each chapter will include topical questions with direct answers. There is no need to read the chapters in order, although they are intended to roughly follow the chronological order you would face them. When applicable the answer will include specific reference to the Arizona law that applies or a website with more information. Many answers are anecdotal and open to variation depending on your experience.

Chapter 1
Initial Matters

The initial days after the death of a loved one may feel like a whirlwind of activity. You may experience a wide range of emotions. Friends and family members may congregate in a manner that few of them are used to, and certainly none of them will be comfortable with. Some people will mourn, some will draw inward, some will bicker, some will find their faith strengthened, and some will sleep all day. Every family is different and every death brings together an unpredictable mix of emotions and personalities. In this context the survivors are asked to make important decisions – decisions that suddenly seem more important and pressing than ever before.

These initial decisions carry emotional weight for the survivors. There are expectations, religious beliefs, and financial issues to consider. The decision maker must consider the expressed desires of the deceased person – which may or may not be in writing – and his or her own opinions. The decision maker is also likely to consider the opinions of other family members and close friends because the decision maker knows that everyone has an opinion whether they share it or not. Even the friendly plea, "It's up to you, Mother," must be examined for underlying bias.

The typical matters that arise immediately after a person's death are predictable:

- Burial vs. cremation
- How to prepare an obituary
- How to honor the deceased person

Of course, there are other issues that arise depending on the situation. For example, the survivors may be asked about organ, tissue, or body donation. But in most cases, the survivors will organize their camp around these three matters.

It usually does not take long for these matters to require decisions. The body must be delivered somewhere. The pastor asks whether a service should be planned. A family member lets everyone know that the deceased person wanted to be cremated. A friend offers to write a draft of the obituary. These issues require action – usually within a few days, or even hours. At worst, the death was a shock to everyone and even asking the questions drops a spark into a furnace burning with stress. At best, the survivors are left with a mix of raw emotions, accompanied by both fatigue and an uncomfortable feeling that a burden has been lifted from the caretakers.

In most cases – but certainly not always – it is fairly obvious who is primarily responsible for making the initial decisions and administering the estate. A surviving spouse will almost always fill this role, although perhaps not if he or she is too elderly or confined to a nursing home. If there is no surviving spouse, then one or more adult children usually step forward. It is difficult to predict how the death of a parent will affect the children emotionally, so it is also difficult to predict which child will gravitate toward the leadership role. If a child lives nearby, and was providing constant care to the parent prior to death, this child tends to seek the leadership role. However, there are other factors, such as birth order, personality, occupation, and flexibility to suddenly take leave from one's place of work.

From a legal perspective, it makes no difference who steps forward into the initial leadership role as long as the correct persons are given the opportunity to make the final decisions. If the surviving spouse is unable to initiate the process, any member of the family or even a knowledgeable social worker or funeral home director can guide the family.

The person or persons taking the initial leadership role must anticipate the impact of raw emotions and varying expectations. The leader may also have to sort through conflicting sets of information about the deceased person's preferences, finances, and estate planning documents.

We are all familiar with the intra-family conflict and tension that arise when extended family members get together for celebrated events, such as holidays, reunions, and marriages. These conflicts and tensions are often multiplied after the death of a family member.

Even in the best scenarios, where family members get along well and carefully manage to celebrate the life of the deceased person, the leader is wise to recognize the possibility of well-intentioned, but nevertheless, poor counsel from family and friends. It is easy for any of us to apply past experience to a new situation without adjusting for new information. The family leader must balance the deceased person's expressed wishes – both written and oral – while seeking consensus from the family. This is no small task when one child says, "I know this is what Dad wanted," or another says, "It's your decision, Mom," with a tone that suggests disapproval for all but the child's preference.

The best counsel is to proceed methodically. Your own grieving process may dictate a slower pace than others may demand. There is no reason you must complete the final arrangements and memorial service within three days of death, even if you are led to believe that is normal. Of course, the initial matters should be handled promptly, but it is better to do things right than quickly should these objectives conflict with each other. If you need a few extra days to grieve, that should be your priority.

Many families have a tendency to believe that prompt action is required in regards to the deceased person's finances. For the vast majority of cases, prompt action is not required. For example, there is no need to schedule a meeting with an estate attorney until at least the final arrangements are complete. Unless there are unusual matters to address, or the family requests advice about how to handle the initial matters, the process of administering the deceased person's financial assets need not begin for several weeks after death. On the other hand, if the person likely to be responsible for administering the estate lives elsewhere, it may be helpful to schedule an initial consultation with an estate attorney before that person travels home.

The balance of this book will assume that you – the reader – have accepted a leadership role in administering an estate. This does not mean that you are solely responsible for handling each task, but it does mean that you will at least help determine who is responsible and help them accomplish the task.

ORGAN AND TISSUE DONATION

Should we consent to organ donation?

Depending on various factors such as the cause of death, you may be informed that your loved one is a candidate for organ or tissue donation. Sometimes this conversation is started before death because the process may require action soon after death. However, if the cause of death was an accident leading to brain death, you may be approached initially about the topic during the difficult hours soon thereafter.

When faced with the possibility of making a donation, the first priority should be to determine the deceased person's wishes. The vast majority of adults have an opinion on this matter, and it may have been expressed to someone during the deceased person's lifetime. This issue is often considered when preparing an estate plan. Many will have a strong preference in favor of donation. Others will be strongly against it, and share a wide array of reasons for having said so.

Your task is to find out whether the deceased person expressed an opinion on the matter during conversation, and if so, then follow it. If you do not already know the answer, then interview family members and friends – even the physician and attorney – because the deceased person may have spoken about the topic to one of them. Survivors commonly recall conversations from many years earlier, which had been forgotten until needed. All of these conversations are helpful, but you should refrain from making a decision until you have searched for other written evidence of the deceased person's wishes. It is certainly not unprecedented for someone to change their opinion on the subject during the final days of life.

Will a driver license include proper consent?

Many people assume that an Arizona driver license is the customary method to record a preference about organ and tissue donation. However, this method was replaced many years ago by the Arizona Donor Registry, which permits initial sign-up and changes to the registrant's preferences via the Internet. Arizona residents may register their preference either online at **www.azdonorregistry.org** or by calling (800) 943-6667.

The Motor Vehicle Division of the Arizona Department of Transportation continues to facilitate the registration process by including a reference to organ and tissue donation on its application form for any driver license, instruction permit, or identification card.

Specifically the form includes a line stating, "I want to be an organ and tissue donor. By checking this box, Donor Network of AZ will add me to the Donate Life AZ Registry." If you select the box, the Motor Vehicle Division will forward your information to the Donor Network of Arizona for registration. The registrant's preference is not printed on the driver license card, but may be noted with a green sticker.

The Arizona Donor Registry is coordinated by the Donor Network of Arizona, which is a federally-designated, non-profit, organ procurement and tissue and eye recovery organization. The Donor Network of Arizona shares organs regionally and nationally through the United Network for Organ Sharing.

A health care provider can determine whether the deceased person registered as a donor by contacting the Donor Network of Arizona. You may also find a card in the deceased person's wallet from the Donor Network. The card is white with a blue stripe across the top and it states, "This card confirms that I've registered my decision to be an organ donor at **www.AZDonorRegistry.org**." If you suspect the deceased person had a strong preference for organ donation, but cannot find evidence, you might also try calling the Donor Network.

Will a power of attorney include proper consent?

Another place you may find the deceased person's preference about organ and tissue donation is a health care power of attorney. Most forms, including the Arizona statutory form, include a section on this topic. The Arizona form states, "Under Arizona law, you may make a gift of all or part of your body to a bank or storage facility or a hospital, physician or medical or dental school for transplantation, therapy, medical or dental evaluation or research or for the advancement of medical or dental science. You may also authorize your agent to do so or a member of your family may make a gift unless you give them notice that you do not want a gift made. In the space below you may make a gift yourself or state that you do not want to make a gift. If you do not complete this section, your agent will have the authority to make a gift of a part of your body pursuant to law." *See ARS 36-3224.* The section about organ and tissue donation is optional, so the health care power of attorney might not indicate a preference.

If you are having trouble locating a health care power of attorney, but you believe the deceased person signed one, then you might also try checking with the Office of the Arizona Secretary of State because it maintains the Arizona Advanced Directive Registry. Although the author's observation is that few people have used – or are even aware of – this registry, you might find a Registry wallet card in the deceased person's possession. If you do find this card, go to **www.azsos.gov**, select "Login to registry," and then enter the User ID and password indicated on the card. Even if you do not find a wallet card, you might also try contacting the Secretary of State's office to request a search by calling (800) 458-5842.

What other methods of proper consent are permitted?

Although participation in the Arizona Donor Registry and statement of preference in a health care power of attorney are the best practices, Arizona law also permits someone to indicate their willingness to donate in a valid will. *See ARS 36-844.* This method is used sparingly because its governing statute is now inconsistent with the statutory health care power of attorney form located in *ARS 36-3224*, which includes a section regarding organ and tissue donation. Since the laws were last revised in 2007, the commonly accepted approach by estate attorneys is to include the preference in a health care power of attorney and not a will.

Because the general legislative intent is to encourage the use of health care advance directives, the author assumes that either a will or health care power of attorney is adequate to indicate intent. To muddy the waters even further, Arizona law also permits someone to indicate willingness to donate by simply telling at least two adults, one of whom is disinterested, during a terminal illness or injury. *See ARS 36-844(A)(3).* From an estate planning perspective, the most effective method is to register via the Internet.

Is organ donation permitted when there is no evidence of the deceased person's wishes?

Arizona law prohibits anyone from authorizing a donation if the deceased person indicated an opposition to it. The evidence of opposition need not be in writing, provided the deceased person told at least two adults, one of whom is a disinterested witness. *See ARS 36-846(A).*

If no qualifying evidence is found of the deceased person's intent, then Arizona law establishes an order of priority for authorizing a donation as follows. *See ARS 36-848(A).*

1. Person designated as Health Care Agent in power of attorney
2. Spouse
3. Adult children
4. Parents
5. Domestic partner
6. Adult siblings
7. Adult grandchildren
8. Grandparents
9. Friend
10. Guardian

If there is more than one member of a class who is entitled to make the decision, then the decision may be made by any member of the class unless that person knows of an objection from another member of the class. If there is an objection, a majority of persons from that class who are reasonably available may make the decision. *See ARS 36-848(B).*

What body parts may be donated?

The following organs may be donated: heart, lungs, liver, kidney, pancreas and small intestine. Also, tissues including skin, bones, veins, heart valves, tendons and ligaments. In some cases, corneal donation is an option. If the deceased person has expressed a willingness to donate, the governing provision may specifically identify the organs or body parts that may be donated.

By default, organs and tissue may be donated for the purpose of transplantation, therapy, research or education. However, many donors will restrict the permission to cover transplant or therapeutic purposes only.

How old is too old?

According to the Donor Network of Arizona, a critical need for organs currently exists in the United States. Today anyone can be considered for organ and/or tissue donation, regardless of age or illness. Medical professionals of the Donor Network will determine whether the condition of organs and tissue is sufficient to permit donation.

AUTOPSY

Who is permitted to order an autopsy?

Prior to issuing a death certificate, the county medical examiner's office must determine the cause of death. When the death occurred in a nursing home or hospital, or at home if the death was anticipated, the cause of death is not difficult to identify and an autopsy is rarely performed.

If the cause of death is more difficult to ascertain, such as when the death occurred rather unexpectedly, a physician may request an autopsy prior to signing the death certificate.

In other situations, certain family members may request an autopsy that would otherwise not occur, provided someone is willing to pay for it. *See ARS 36-832(A).* The autopsy cannot occur without proper consent. Under *ARS 36-3224*, the deceased person may give this authority to a person designated in a health care power of attorney. Absent such designation or the presence of any surviving family members, the person who accepts responsibility for final arrangements may consent to the autopsy. *See ARS 36-832(B).*

WHOLE BODY DONATION

Who accepts whole body donations in Arizona?

In some cases a deceased person may have wanted his or her whole body to be donated for education and research. This process requires some quick decision making after death, so most people interested in body donation will register themselves prior to death and then tell several close family members so they know who to call immediately after death.

The rules in Arizona regarding whole body donations are the same as for donation of organs and tissue. If the deceased person did not state a preference regarding whole body donation, the person or persons with priority under Arizona law may do so. *See ARS 36-848(A).* Arizona law permits whole body donation over objection by some family members, however organizations are likely to decline a donation when a family member raises an objection.

There are several large organizations that accept whole body donations. These include Science Care, Biological Resource Center, Mayo Clinic, and Med Cure. You should be able to find information about these and others by searching for the term "whole body donation in Arizona" in any popular Internet search engine.

If a local organization is preferred, contact the College of Medicine Willed Body Program at the University of Arizona. The program will accept whole body donations primarily for medical education, and to a lesser extent, research purposes at the university medical campuses in both Tucson and Phoenix. The only cost is a transportation fee, but currently this is waived for bodies transported from Pima, Pinal and Maricopa counties. For more information, visit **www.bodydonation.med.arizona.edu** or call (520) 626-6083.

How do I know whether the body will be accepted?

You will need to call one of the organizations within 24 hours of death. With prior registration, most bodies are accepted. Typical disqualifications include HIV/AIDS, hepatitis B and C, active tuberculosis and syphilis. Other conditions will require increased scrutiny include severe obesity, decomposition, trauma, and extensive orthopedic surgeries.

Some organizations, including the University of Arizona, will not accept whole body donations if any organs or tissue were removed for donation purposes.

FINAL ARRANGEMENTS

What if there are prearrangements for burial or cremation?

Absent whole body donation, the deceased person's body may be buried or cremated. In some cases, the deceased person will have prearranged a burial or cremation so there are few decisions for the survivors to make. The process may be as simple as contacting the mortuary and arranging for it to remove the body from the place of death. The mortuary will proceed to carry out the plan assuming payment was accounted for prior to death.

If you are not sure whether the deceased person made prearrangements, then ask family members and friends whom the deceased person may have spoken to about the subject. When prearrangements are made, the mortuary usually gives a folder to the client with copies of the contract and other information. You should look for that folder with the deceased person's other important papers. If the deceased person had an estate plan drawn up by an estate attorney, you might also contact the law firm to ask whether any information about prearrangement was recorded there. Otherwise, you will have to make all of the final arrangements with a mortuary of your choice.

Is cremation an option?

The survivors may arrange for cremation of the body, provided the deceased person did not indicate a preference for burial.

Studies show that Arizona has one of the highest rates of cremation in the United States. Approximately 65% of all deceased bodies in Arizona are cremated, and it is estimated that the number approaches 75% in the metro areas of Phoenix and Tucson.

In Arizona, the typical cost is $750 to $1,250 for direct cremation and a simple urn. Although costs of a funeral and transportation of the body may increase the overall expense, a funeral package including cremation is almost always less expensive than burial.

Must we honor the known wishes of the deceased person?

Yes, you must follow the deceased person's direction if it is reasonable and does not impose a substantial burden on the authorized decision maker. *See ARS 36-831.01(A)*. Obviously, this is a difficult law to interpret and enforce. A mortuary may lean naturally toward the direction of the authorized decision maker even when the direction appears to conflict with the deceased person's wishes. After all, it is the authorized decision maker who must locate the resources to make payment.

Perhaps a better way to explain this is to ask how someone could prearrange a burial or cremation and know that it could not be changed at the direction of surviving family members.

Under Arizona law, a prearranged burial or cremation is not binding unless the deceased person contracted for payment. In other words, it is possible for someone to set up a file at a mortuary, but choose not to pay for it ahead of time. Thus, the only way to prearrange a burial or cremation and be sure that it will be carried out is to arrange for payment. But even that may not be enough. A mortuary could theoretically refuse to proceed if the deceased person failed to sign a provision commonly referred to as an "immunity document."

This provision releases the mortuary from liability when honoring a deceased person's wishes, even when there are family members who refuse to consent to the final arrangements preferred by the deceased person. Without this signed provision, in theory, the person otherwise responsible for authorizing the final arrangements could choose burial even when the deceased person established a plan for cremation with the mortuary.

Mortuaries vary in their use and presentation of an immunity document. When making prearrangements, it may be necessary to ask about it. The provision may also go by another name. For example, a prominent Tucson mortuary refers to the document as a "Notice Regarding Disposition of Remains." The basis for the Immunity Document is *ARS 32-1365.01*, which states, "A legally competent adult may prepare a written statement directing the cremation or other lawful disposition of the legally competent adult's own remains pursuant to section 36-831." If the document is properly signed and witnessed, a mortuary may proceed to carry out the wishes of the deceased person without obtaining authorization from anyone.

Who has the authority to make the final arrangements?

After a death it is not unusual for several family members to make the trip to a local mortuary. Of course, the process of bringing extended family members together to plan and pay for final arrangements will test even the best family relations. A counselor for the mortuary will need to determine who is authorized to make final decisions. Traditionally this right belongs to the "next of kin," but the answer may first depend on what the deceased person's estate plan says.

As described in the prior section, if the deceased person prearranged the details of a burial or cremation, and made financial arrangements to carry them out, then it is not difficult to proceed. If the mortuary is in possession of a signed authorization under *ARS 32-1365.01*, then it is permitted to proceed without any further review. Otherwise, the mortuary will have to obtain proper authorization.

Arizona law establishes a specific order of priority for who may authorize the final arrangements as follows. *See ARS 36-831.*

1. Surviving spouse
2. Person designated as having power of attorney
3. Adult children
4. Parent
5. Adult sibling
6. Adult grandchild
7. Grandparent
8. Adult friend

As a practical matter, there are a few exceptions. For example, a mortuary will generally seek unanimous consent from all of the family members or at least from those who can be located and choose to be involved with the arrangements. Also, a surviving spouse will be disqualified if the couple was legally separated or a petition for divorce was pending at the time of death.

Note that because the surviving spouse has first priority, it is not possible to "disinherit" a spouse from this position. Even if the spouse is very elderly, he or she will have first priority unless the mortuary is presented with evidence that the spouse is unable or unwilling to make the necessary decisions.

The next priority is to the person designated as having power of attorney. The statute clarifies that authority may be conferred on either a health care or financial power of attorney; provided, however, the document specifically gives the person the authority to make decisions regarding final arrangements. In Arizona, it is customary to include this provision in a health care power of attorney because *ARS 36-3224* includes an optional provision regarding final arrangements in its sample health care power of attorney form.

Absent a surviving spouse to handle the arrangements, it is very common for a person to designate an adult child as agent in a health care power of attorney. Under Arizona law, the adult child named in a health care power of attorney clearly has priority over any other adult children. However, a mortuary acting cautiously may seek the unanimous consent (or at least a majority) of the adult children before proceeding.

What happens when the adult children cannot agree or when one of them cannot be found?

If the decision regarding final arrangements falls to the deceased person's adult children, for example, and they cannot agree, then the mortuary may proceed upon obtaining consent from a majority of the children who are reasonably available. *See ARS 36-831(D).* A reasonable attempt to contact all of the children is required. In theory, if a majority cannot be reached after considerable effort, the person next in priority could break the tie. However, a mortuary may refuse to proceed entirely.

From an estate planning perspective, the better approach is to designate one person as agent for final arrangements in a health care power of attorney. For this reason most health care powers of attorney drafted by estate attorneys in Arizona now specifically refer to *ARS 36-831* in the document.

What if final arrangements are made but someone later argues the wrong choice was made?

Under Arizona law, the authorized decision maker is immune from liability provided a reasonable effort was made to determine the deceased person's wishes prior to making the decision. *See ARS 36-831(H).*

What if the deceased person's power of attorney failed to include a preference regarding final arrangements?

There is some debate whether a person designated as agent in a health care power of attorney may authorize final arrangements when the document does not specifically refer to the power. A cautious mortuary is unlikely to accept authorization from a health care agent unless the document includes specific language on this subject. This affects older power of attorney documents because the applicable law was amended in 2007. Many health care powers of attorney drafted both before and after the law was established fail to include specific provisions. Documents drafted using self-help legal software and form books are even less likely to include this language.

If the deceased person signed a health care power of attorney without specific reference to *ARS 36-831*, the result is open to independent interpretation. What if an adult child is the designated power of attorney, but another adult child is present who objects?

The author's interpretation is to disregard the health care agent, at least to that person's capacity as health care agent, because *ARS 36-831(A)(2)* states that specific authority must be mentioned in the power of attorney document. The mortuary should require authorization by at least a majority of the adult children based on the statute. Many people who sign a health care power of attorney fail to recognize its implication toward final arrangements. Unless the document specifically mentions final arrangements, the power of attorney should be disregarded.

If so desired a properly drafted health care power of attorney should now include a statement of this nature: "My health care agent shall be responsible for burial, funeral and other disposition arrangements under ARS Section 36-831." Absent this provision you should not be surprised if the mortuary refuses to proceed without authorization from all of the persons in the class with highest priority under *ARS 36-831(A)*.

A similar issue is presented when the deceased person left a valid health care power of attorney under the laws of another state, but died in Arizona. Similarly, a cautious mortuary is unlikely to honor this power of attorney.

What if the power of attorney designates co-agents who disagree with each other?

This is yet another issue that may be interpreted inconsistently by mortuaries. For most priority classes in the statute, any member may serve as the authorizing agent if the member is unaware of any objection by another member of the class. Otherwise, a majority of the class can act. However, *ARS 36-831(D)* curiously excludes the power of attorney category from these general rules. Thus, if the health care power of attorney designates two or more persons as co-agents, then it is the author's interpretation that all must agree in order to authorize the final arrangements. Unfortunately, many people who complete powers of attorney without the counsel of an estate attorney will designate two or more persons as co-agents. This drafting choice is rarely helpful and may often complicate the situation. The statute and legislative history do not appear to consider the possibility of co-agents in a power of attorney.

How do we pay for final arrangements when estate funds are restricted?

Although the estate is ultimately responsible for payment, it is possible that no one will have access to funds of the estate until several days or weeks after the burial or cremation. Thus, the survivors may be asked to pay the mortuary at time of service. The mortuary is running a business, of course, so it should be easy to understand its concern for getting paid.

If funds are difficult to access, the simplest option is for a family member to pay the invoice by credit card. The expense can be reimbursed by the estate at a later date.

When there are no survivors willing and able to pay the invoice, there are two additional options, which you may have to inquire about. First, you can request financing through the estate. Most mortuaries will provide the personal representative (or trustee) with a certain number of days to pay the invoice without having to pay any additional fees. Interest and fees would accrue after that date. In this case the mortuary becomes one of the highest priority creditors of the estate funds. Second, you can request a bank or credit union where the deceased person held an account to cut a cashier's check directly from the account to the mortuary. The author has found banks sympathetic to this situation when asked. They are often willing to make this payment without presentation of a certified death certificate as long as some other proof of death is provided to the bank.

How do we pay for final arrangements when the estate has no assets?

If the deceased person died without any assets available to pay for the final arrangements, then anyone may pay the costs out-of-pocket. If the estate later is solvent, the cost may be reimbursed.

Each county has a contract with one or more mortuaries to provide low-cost, direct cremations. If you have to pay out-of-pocket, you should ask for a list of these contracted mortuaries in order to minimize the expense.

But what if no one is willing or able to pay? If the deceased person was an honorably discharged veteran or the surviving spouse of one, then the county will notify the veteran's administration or a local veteran's organization, or both, of the death and give the organization the opportunity to provide for the final arrangements. Otherwise, the county will handle the cremation at taxpayer expense. The mortuary is assigned on a rotation basis by the medical examiner's office. Eligibility is based on income and assets of the deceased person and next of kin and must meet federal poverty guidelines. If the county subsequently learns of money held in an account owned by the deceased person, it may file an affidavit with the financial institution and get reimbursed.

How do we arrange for transportation of the remains outside Arizona?

If you decide to transport the deceased person's casketed or cremated remains outside the state of Arizona, you will need to obtain a Disposition-Transit Permit. *See ARS 36-326.* A mortuary can obtain this permit on your behalf and handle all necessary transportation arrangements.

You should take a death certificate along with you in the event you need to pass through a security checkpoint.

If you intend to take the urn on an airplane, remember that the urn must pass through an x-ray machine like any other luggage item, whether part of carry-on or checked baggage. The Transportation Security Administration (TSA) will not open the urn, but will inspect its contents and urn materials using its normal equipment. Be sure to check with the airline before making your reservation because some do not permit urns to be transported onboard and/or in checked baggage.

Some urns are made of material that generates an opaque image and prevents the x-ray from working properly. Most wood or plastic urns will pass without issue, but visit the TSA website for more information on what materials are not acceptable. If the cremated remains will be stored in an urn that is not acceptable by the TSA, they suggest using a temporary urn made from wood or plastic. More information is available at **www.tsa.gov**.

MILITARY BURIAL

Where are the military cemeteries in Arizona?

If the deceased person was an honorably discharged veteran of the United States military, or if the deceased person was a surviving spouse or dependent child of a veteran, the deceased person's body may be buried in a national military cemetery. For more detailed eligibility information, visit **www.cem.va.gov/cem/burial_benefits/eligible.asp**. Family members may be buried in a national military cemetery even if the eligible service member is still alive.

Located in northern Phoenix, the National Memorial Cemetery of Arizona has space available to accommodate casketed and cremated remains. If you want to schedule a burial, send all discharge documentation by fax to the national scheduling office at (866) 900-6417 and follow up with a phone call to (800) 535-1117. For more information about the Phoenix facility, visit **www.cem.va.gov/CEMs/nchp/nmca.asp** or call the cemetery directly at (480) 513-3600.

The second national cemetery in Arizona is located in Prescott. It is closed to new casket burials although they will accommodate casketed remains of subsequent family members in the same gravesite of previously interred family members. In addition, they have space for cremated remains in a columbarium. For more information about the Prescott facility, visit **www.cem.va.gov/cems/nchp/prescott.asp** or call the cemetery at (480) 513-3600.

The National Memorial Cemetery of Arizona has a full time Honor Guard made up of representatives of local veterans service organizations.

Upon request, they will provide a 10-15 minute non-denominational service, rifle salute, and playing of Taps.

In addition, there is a military cemetery operated by the Arizona Department of Veterans' Services in Sierra Vista. The application for interment is on their website at **http://dvs.az.gov/services/cemetery.aspx** or by calling (520) 458-7144. The Southern Arizona Veterans' Memorial Cemetery is not intended for traditional services, but a brief military honor service is provided.

A final option is the Arlington National Cemetery outside Washington DC. The eligibility rules and cost allocation are the same as Arizona cemeteries. However, you are responsible for the entire cost of transporting the casketed or cremated remains to Arlington.

Will the VA handle all final arrangements for free?

No. This is a common misunderstanding. The Department of Veterans Affairs does not make funeral arrangements or perform cremations. The survivors are responsible for making these arrangements with a funeral or cremation provider. The VA cemeteries are intended solely to provide space for casketed and cremated remains. Transportation to the cemetery is also not included.

Other benefits available from the VA cemeteries include a government headstone or marker, a burial flag, and a Presidential Memorial Certificate. These benefits are also available at no cost if the deceased person's body is buried at a private cemetery.

However, in certain circumstances, the Veterans Benefits Administration will provide a burial allowance. If the death was not service-related, then the deceased person's estate may qualify for up to $700 toward burial and funeral expenses and an additional $700 for plot interment. This benefit should not be confused with the $255 death benefit from Social Security Administration. If the death occurred while the veteran was in a VA hospital or under VA contracted nursing home care, some or all of the costs for transporting the veteran's remains may be reimbursed. The allowance must be applied for by filling out VA Form 21-530. More information is available at the VA website.

DEATH CERTIFICATES

How many death certificates do we need?

The mortuary will provide information to the health department in the county where the death occurred in order to obtain a death certificate. When all of the required information is presented, including cause of death, the Office of Vital Records will create and issue a death certificate. Upon registration, you should order several certified copies of the death certificate.

It is difficult to predict how many certified copies you will need to administer the estate. You can obtain a rough estimate by adding the number of real estate properties owned by the deceased person, plus the number of investment accounts and life insurance policies, then add one or two just in case. This decision almost always creates more stress than what it is worth, especially because it is simple to order additional copies for $20 each. Note that a mortuary may add a service fee to make the initial order.

If you need to order additional certified copies of the death certificate, you will need to contact the Office of Vital Records. If the death occurred within the last 30 days, you may be able to obtain certified copies at a local office in the county where the death occurred. For a list of county offices, visit **www.azdhs.gov**. If the death occurred more than 30 days ago, you can apply in person at the State Office of Vital Records in Phoenix, by mail, or through **www.vitalchek.com**. The Vital Chek service includes a service fee, but the expedited service option may be worth the extra cost.

OBITUARY

How do we publish an obituary?

A local newspaper will usually publish a record of the deceased person's death based on its access to public records – whether you request it or not. However, if you wish to publish an obituary, you will need to choose a newspaper and submit an application. The best place to start is to visit **www.legacy.com**. They will provide a list of newspapers and help you submit the obituary. In general, normal classified ad rates for the newspaper will apply. Of course, you can publish multiple obituaries. For example, you might publish one in Arizona and another in the deceased person's hometown back in the Midwest. Another option is to create a memorial website using **www.legacy.com** or another similar website.

There are books and online services to help you write the obituary. However, the best approach is to let someone in the family with some writing skills prepare a first draft. Others can make suggested improvements before the final draft is produced. In addition, the vast majority of newspapers now permit online eulogies where anyone can post an entry remembering the deceased person.

MINOR CHILDREN

Who takes guardianship of a surviving minor child?

If the deceased person is survived by one or more minor children (under age 18), then an adult relative or close friend of the family should take temporary custody of the children until a formal guardianship appointment is made by the court where the minor resides.

In this event the welfare of the child is likely to be the top priority so there may be several people willing to take temporary custody. If the deceased parent is survived by an ex-spouse who is also the parent of the child, Arizona law will presume the parent is entitled to custody rights absent extraordinary evidence. Family members of the deceased parent may have other ideas, of course, so tread cautiously if this is the case. A judge may frown on any attempts to keep the child from a biological parent, even for a short time.

If the situation is complicated, you should bring the matter immediately to a local family law attorney who can help petition for a court-appointed temporary guardian. The temporary guardianship lasts for a set amount of time, or until a permanent guardian is appointed.

If there is some question about who should have temporary custody, check to see if the deceased parent nominated a guardian in a valid will. For the initial days after death, it may not be possible to have the named guardian take custody yet, but certainly that is an option.

After the other initial matters are complete, the prospective guardian should consult with a local family law attorney to begin the process of formal guardianship proceedings. If the deceased person's will nominated a guardian, and that person is willing and able to accept the responsibility, then the probate judge is likely to appoint that person formally as the guardian. On the other hand, if the child has attained age 14, the child can object to the appointment. A judge will then give significant weight to the child's choice of guardian before ultimately making an appointment in the best interests of the child. *See ARS 14-5201 et. al.*

VICTIMS OF CRIME COMPENSATION FUND

Does the State provide any compensation for the family members of a crime victim?

The Arizona Criminal Justice Commission administers a program to reimburse crime victims and their families who suffer losses not covered by insurance, public funds, or any other compensation. The program can cover crime-related expenses for medical costs, mental health counseling, funerals, wage loss, and crime scene clean-up. For more information and conditions of eligibility, visit **www.azcjc.gov/ACJC.Web/victim/VictComp.aspx**.

Chapter 2

Get Organized

A fter the busy days immediately following the death of a loved one, it is natural to lose some of the initial motivation to administer the estate. Most friends and extended family members drop back into their regular life routines, while the closest survivors are left to deal with the legal and financial issues ahead. Accordingly, the process of administering an estate usually appears most daunting at this time and procrastination makes a tempting choice. However, it is very important that someone take formal responsibility for the protection of property. Even a relatively simple estate administration can seem overwhelming when the death was unexpected or not planned for. Especially if the estate includes a wide variety of assets, this process requires someone with organizational skills or at least a delegation of responsibility to someone who can offer these skills. The objective is to gather as much information as possible and begin to establish order to the administration process.

At this stage the most common question asked to an estate attorney is whether probate is necessary. Many people mistakenly assume that probate is unnecessary when there is a surviving spouse and usually necessary when there is not. Both assumptions may be incorrect, but regardless, the question is premature. The critical step of gathering information about the assets and liabilities in the estate must occur before an estate attorney can determine whether a probate is needed. Although the beneficiaries may not want to hear it, the best approach is to take things slow. Some of the most common errors in estate administration are committed by survivors who rush this step and fail to obtain a complete understanding of the estate before paying debts or making distributions to the beneficiaries.

What property deserves immediate attention?

Some types of assets should be located and secured as soon as possible. If the estate will be administered by a surviving spouse, this process is usually not difficult. But if not, the estate administrator should begin a search for sensitive items and secure them appropriately. Obvious items include the deceased person's wallet and credit cards. Others include cell phones, computers, car keys, garage door openers, firearms, and pets. The estate may also include valuable personal property such as antiques, fine china, or jewelry. All of these items should be found and secured.

If a residence has been left vacant, it must be secured immediately. You may want to consider retaining a locksmith to re-key the door locks. Similarly, if a residence has an alarm system, a cautious administrator will program a new access code to prevent unauthorized entry. A search should be made around the house for keys of all types. Also, check with neighbors to see if the deceased person left a spare house key with any of them. At some point the estate administrator will need to determine the purpose of each key. But at this point the objective is simply to gather and secure all of them.

Unless a motor vehicle is titled jointly with a surviving person, motor vehicles belonging to the deceased person should be used rarely. The estate is liable for property damage or bodily injury resulting from use of the car. Be sure to contact the insurance company and verify that coverage is ongoing. If the coverage is about to end, you should make arrangements to pay the premium for the next period. A refund will be available if the motor vehicle is sold before the end of the period.

Be sure to search the residence, motor vehicles, and personal belongings for prescription medications. You may need to look in jackets, desk drawers, and medicine cabinets. These should be collected and stored in a secure location until they be disposed of properly at a later date.

Other assets that will require immediate attention include businesses and rental properties. Some may already have ongoing professional management, but many will not. Employees may need direction on how to proceed, and assurance that they will be paid in a timely manner. Affected clients, customers, vendors, and tenants may present immediate and urgent tasks that must be addressed. At minimum, affected parties should know who to contact in order to address their needs in the short term.

What documents should I be looking for?

You should look carefully for any estate planning documents. It is possible, of course, that none will be found, but that should not prevent anyone from looking. On the other hand, some people retain old estate planning documents unnecessarily. Collect all copies you can find.

If you have ever completed an estate plan for yourself, you probably know what to look for. The most obvious document is a will. Although most wills are prepared by attorneys and witnessed by at least two adults, you should keep an eye out for handwritten wills, also known as holographic wills. In Arizona, even a handwritten note may qualify as a will provided it meets some basic requirements. A holographic will must be signed by the deceased person, but no witnesses are required. *See ARS 14-2503*. In some cases, there may be a handwritten document without sufficient detail to qualify as a valid will. Although some of its content might be helpful to clarify intent, you should disregard the provisions of such a document.

Other documents to look for include trust agreements (also referred to as "Declarations of Trust"), and papers regarding life insurance policies, annuities, and retirement accounts. If you have access to the appropriate passwords, you might also try to sign into financial accounts via the Internet and monitor the deceased person's e-mail account. This will permit you to start putting the financial puzzle together so you can determine how to proceed.

Surveys show that approximately one-half of adults do not have a valid estate plan, although a smaller percentage of adults actually die without one. A person who dies without a valid will dies "intestate" – the opposite of "testate" which means to die with a valid will. However, someone who dies intestate may have other documents besides a will that govern the distribution of assets, such as a life insurance beneficiary designation. You should assume that every life insurance policy, annuity, and retirement account has a beneficiary designation on file, so if you cannot find one in the deceased person's possessions, then you will need to inquire of the various financial institutions.

Other important documents to look for include a social security card, passport, paystubs, and membership cards. Some documents may be kept in a fireproof box or safe deposit box. If you cannot access the fireproof box, you may need to hire a locksmith to open it. Unfortunately, this may require proof of death and perhaps proof of your authority to open it, something you may not have until later in the estate administration process.

Many savvy elderly persons know that the freezer is an excellent place to store documents because emergency medical technicians often check there for health care powers of attorney and living wills. You should check there too.

What can I do in the home before someone is appointed to administer the estate?

If you are the person responsible for administering the estate, and you do not live in the deceased person's home, then you will need to take steps to secure it. The first step is to gain entry into the home and take a look around. It is always a good idea to take photographs or video of the contents of the home before you touch anything. Check that no water is running, the windows are locked, and keep a light on at night. If you feel the home may be insecure, contact a locksmith or the apartment manager to re-key the locks. You may be surprised to learn how many friends and family members – well intentioned or not – try to enter a deceased person's home.

You may discover the house has an alarm system. This is a helpful protective device, but you may have some difficulty using a system that you are not accustomed to. Contact the alarm company, explain the situation, and request to meet with a technician who will explain how it works and help you program a new code. The alarm company might require a death certificate and proof that you have authority to access the residence. This may delay the process, so you should inquire by phone about what steps they require to prove authority. Although you may be tempted to keep the current code, the better approach is to program a new code so you can control access to the home.

Be sure to clean up the exterior of the home so it is not obviously vacant. Sometimes if the deceased person was not living in the home for a while before death, this requires a lot of clean-up. If this is the case, you might consider calling the deceased person's church, if appropriate, and asking whether it can send a service team to assist with this project.

All perishable items should be removed from the refrigerator and freezer. You may choose to donate these items to a local food bank or perhaps the food pantry at the deceased person's church.

If you must clean a private residence – as opposed to an apartment with a public trash dumpster – then you may want to learn the schedule for regular trash pickup. If necessary, ask a neighbor, call the management company, or search the Internet for information from the trash removal provider.

You will probably be tempted to start dealing with all the stuff in the home. However, it is usually best to let more time pass before doing that. The higher priority should be looking for important papers, but you should hold off on moving any furniture and household items until someone has been appointed formally to administer the estate.

If you have access to the mailbox, make sure that someone checks the mail periodically until a forwarding request can be submitted to the Post Office.

If a pet lives in the home, you may need to retain help from someone to care for the pet until a new home can be found.

ACCESS THE SAFE DEPOSIT BOX

Where do I look for a safe deposit box?

Some important documents and assets may be kept in a safe deposit box at a bank. Thus, you may need to inquire at the banks where the deceased person had accounts whether there are any to inspect. Many estate attorneys suggest that clients do not keep estate planning documents in a safe deposit box, yet some clients do so anyway. On the other hand, it is very possible that you will not find one. Personal safes kept in closets or under desks are probably more common.

How do I access a safe deposit box?

If you have reason to believe the deceased person had a safe deposit box, then inquire with each bank where the deceased person had accounts. For best results, contact the branch manager at the location where you believe the safe deposit box is located. If you learn there is a safe deposit box, then ask if anyone else besides the deceased person is named on the rental contract. If yes, then you must enlist the help of that person to inspect the box.

If there is no other person named on the rental contract, the branch manager may choose to grant access to you under the right circumstances. Your chances of entry are higher if the deceased person was a longtime customer of the bank and the branch manager believes that you are the person responsible for administering the estate. If many cases, the bank will release the entire contents of the safe deposit box to you and close it permanently.

However, the branch manager may prefer to follow the formal procedure described by Arizona law. *See ARS 6-1008*. Upon proof of death, generally by presentation of death certificate, two employees of the bank will open the safe deposit box in the presence of any person who claims to be interested in the contents. It should be emphasized that any person can make this request because it may be impossible to know who is ultimately responsible for administration of the estate until after the safe deposit box is opened. Thus, if you believe yourself to be the person that will administer the estate, then it is good practice to access the safe deposit box as soon as possible.

If the formal procedure is used, employees of the bank may remove any document which appears to be a will and arrange for its delivery to the clerk of the local probate court. Alternatively, the bank has discretion under Arizona law to give the will directly to any person named in the document as personal representative.

In addition, the bank has discretion to remove any life insurance policies from the safe deposit box and deliver them to the named beneficiaries. However, all other contents must be retained by the bank until a personal representative has been appointed or identified.

What if the bank refuses to permit access to the safe deposit box?

No matter how hard you try, the formal procedure described by Arizona law may not be enough to gain access to a safe deposit box. Although rare, the author has observed situations where a bank has exercised its discretion to prohibit any access to a safe deposit box until it receives written authorization in the form of Letters of Personal Representative certified by a probate court. This can be a difficult problem to overcome because the safe deposit box may contain the will that would be used to petition for appointment of a personal representative.

The other challenging situation you might encounter is where the bank permits limited access to search for a will and life insurance policies, but refuses to part with the remaining contents of the safe deposit box without written authorization from the probate court.

In the first case, a letter or call from an estate attorney should do the trick. Absent some extraordinary reason, a branch manager is likely to empathize with someone who has reason to believe the original will is located in the safe deposit box. However, the second case can present an expensive problem. If the estate does not otherwise require a probate action, then the estate administrator is faced with the prospect of petitioning for appointment as personal representative with the probate court for the sole purpose of accessing the remaining contents of the safe deposit box. In both cases described, no one will be happy with the result, especially if the safe deposit box is empty when it is finally opened.

If you are fairly certain a probate action will not be required, the better option is to present an Affidavit for Collection of Personal Property. *See ARS 14-3971(B).* This technique is described more fully in Chapter 5. This will not work in every case, but in most cases will provide the necessary authority under Arizona law to obtain the remaining contents of the safe deposit box.

After reading this section, you may think that gaining access to a safe deposit box is difficult. Actually banks in Arizona are becoming more lenient when asked to release the contents after a death. If the branch manager is comfortable with you and the timing of your request is reasonable, the bank is likely to honor it. It is not in the best interest of the bank to annoy a potential customer when there is no clear reason to block an attempt to settle an estate.

NOTIFY APPROPRIATE COMPANIES AND AGENCIES

After someone dies, there is a long list of people, companies, and organizations to notify about the death. The list varies widely, of course, but there are several that apply in almost all cases.

How do I forward the mail?

If the deceased person's residence is left vacant, the estate administrator will want to arrange for mail forwarding. This requires going to a local post office in person. Although a typical forwarding request can be handled via the Internet, it is the policy of the U.S. Postal Service to require the estate administrator to present Form 3575 and additional documentation in person at a local post office branch. The author is aware of situations where an out-of-state administrator submitted the necessary documentation to the local post office by mail, but this method may not work.

Absent a very friendly post office clerk who is willing to bend the rules a little, you will not be able to forward the mail until you can present a death certificate and demonstrate that you have legal authority to receive the mail. This may take a few weeks after the death, of course, so make sure someone is stopping by regularly to pick up the mail until then. The mailbox may require a key, so you might have to look around for it. If you do not live in the same area as the deceased person, you may want to ask a neighbor or nearby relative to check the mail regularly until you can arrange for mail forwarding.

When you are ready to forward the mail, you should bring a death certificate along with appropriate documentation to prove your authority. If your appointment as Personal Representative was required, you should bring a certified copy of the Letters of Personal Representative. If your appointment was not required, but there is a valid will, then you should present a copy of the will and highlight the section that nominates you as the personal representative. Alternatively, if there was no valid will, then you should identify yourself as the next of kin to the post office clerk when you present the death certificate. All of these techniques should be adequate to permit mail forwarding.

If the post office clerk refuses to forward mail for some reason, then try submitting an Affidavit for Collection of Personal Property as your legal authority. *See ARS 14-3971(B).*

The post office clerk will likely copy the documents you bring in and return the originals to you.

In addition to gathering the necessary estate documents, you should fill out Form 3575 (Change of Address card) before stepping up to the counter. This form is available in the lobby of the post office.

Assuming you have provided adequate documentation, the post office will send you a Change of Address Confirmation to the new address and let you know what date you can expect mail to start forwarding. Newspapers and magazines will be forwarded for at least two months.   First class, priority, and express mail (including packages) will be forwarded for a period of at least one year, which gives you plenty of time to close out the estate.

How do I remove the deceased person's name from direct mail solicitation lists?

The Direct Marketing Association now permits registration of the name of a deceased person on its Deceased Do Not Contact list (DDNC). The DMA initiated this service because it had often received requests from family members, friends, or caretakers seeking to remove the names of deceased persons from marketing lists. You can complete the registration online at **https://www.ims-dm.com/cgi/ddnc.php.**

When should I notify the utility companies?

For any real estate owned by the deceased person, you may need to contact the various utility companies servicing the property. Of course, if the deceased person is survived by another resident whose name is on the account, all this task may require is a phone call to the utility's customer service department in order to remove the deceased person's name. However, you may need to change the account if the surviving resident's name was not on the account, or if you intend to sell or transfer the property to someone else.

If the property is going to be listed for sale, then you will want to keep the electric on. You may not have access to estate funds right away, so you may have to let the account become delinquent for a short time; perhaps three to four weeks maximum. However, do not risk the possibility that the electric company will shut off service even temporarily. If you still do not have access to funds after several weeks, then you should make a payment from your own funds and reimburse yourself later. Unless you anticipate a swift sale or transfer, you should call the electric company to change the account ownership. The bills can be sent to you directly rather than to the deceased person's last address. The electric company might insist that your name be on the title of the account, however the recorded deed is evidence of ownership. You are not personally responsible for payment of the electric bill. Don't worry about the exact titling of the account, which does not matter much.

On the other hand, if you do anticipate a swift sale or transfer, then you might choose to refrain from contacting the electric company until the new resident moves in and transfers the service.

Further, it is common for elderly persons to establish a budget billing program where the monthly payment is fixed year-round. Budget billing usually leaves a credit at death, so you may need to request a refund. You can find out whether budget billing was used simply by reviewing recent bank statements to see if the monthly amount was fixed.

Similar advice is appropriate for the water, trash, and gas companies, if applicable. If the house is going to be listed for sale, you may want these services to continue. A potential home buyer may want these services on, and a home inspection would require it.

If the deceased person rented an apartment, then you should call to terminate the utility accounts as soon as the apartment is vacated.

Should I cancel the cable TV?

If the deceased person had cable TV or satellite service (e.g., DirectTV), then you should call immediately to cancel the service. In some cases, you may need to meet a technician at the property to arrange for shutdown of the signal or return of satellite property. If this is a scheduling hardship for you, you might ask a neighbor, close relative, or college student who needs some extra house-sitting income to wait for the technician. Otherwise, ask the listing real estate agent if they might stay at the property during that time – perhaps using the time as an open house if the property is ready. Ask the customer service representative if they will send the final bill directly to you. If not, then you can still get the final bill by waiting for the mail to be forwarded to you. In most cases, these customer service representatives will be eager to work with you.

What should I do with the deceased person's credit cards?

Be sure to locate all of the deceased person's credit cards. If you find it difficult to gain access to the checking account right away, you may be tempted to use the credit card for some expenses. Do not do this. It is illegal unless you are an authorized signer on the account. The better approach is to use your own credit card and reimburse yourself later.

You should call the customer service department for each credit card – usually listed on the back of the card – and notify them of the cardholder's death. If there is another cardholder on the account, then be sure to emphasize not to cancel the account, but rather just the card associated with the deceased account holder. Then cut the deceased person's credit cards, but save the pieces in a small sandwich bag for a time until you are confident that all cards have been found.

Will Social Security payments stop automatically?

The mortuary will likely inform the Social Security Administration office about the death. However, you may verify this has been done by calling (800) 772-1213. You will need to provide the deceased person's social security number and date of birth when you call.

If the deceased person was receiving a regular monthly benefit from Social Security, then you may need to return the last payment. Each payment represents the prior month's benefit, but it assumes the beneficiary survived the entire month. In other words, any payment received after the month when the death occurred must be returned. For example, if a deposit is made on August 3 after the beneficiary died on July 14, then the August payment must be returned. On the other hand, if the beneficiary died on August 1, the payment may be kept.

Since it takes several days to process a Notice of Death, the Social Security Administration may send payment after the date of your call. You can sometimes predict whether this will happen based on the day of the month on which the beneficiary receives the payment. Generally, the date of the month on which the beneficiary receives the benefit depends on the birth date of the person on whose record the beneficiary receives the benefits. If the beneficiary received benefits as a spouse, the payment date is determined by the spouse's birth date. For example, if the deceased person received a monthly Social Security benefit as a retired worker, and whose birth date is between 1 and 10, then the date of payment is the second Wednesday. Likewise, if the birth date is between 11 and 20, then the payment is made on the third Wednesday; and if the birth date is between 21 and 31, then the fourth Wednesday.

There are exceptions, of course. If the beneficiary was already receiving a Social Security benefit prior to May 1997, then the payment may still occur on the third day of the month. Similarly, if the beneficiary also received a SSI benefit, then the Social Security payment is made on the third day of the month and the SSI payment is made on the first day of the month.

Most beneficiaries receive payment by electronic deposit to a bank account. You should contact the bank or financial institution where the payment is deposited, notify them of the death, and request that any funds received for the month of death and later be returned to Social Security as soon as possible. Even if you fail to do this, the Social Security Administration may eventually determine there was an overpayment, and will withdraw the amount electronically from the account. Either way, you should be careful not to close the account until this has occurred, which may take several weeks.

What survivor benefits are available through Social Security?

Eligible spouses and dependent children are eligible to receive $255 in order to offset burial expenses. If eligible, the mortuary may complete the application and apply the payment directly to its bill for services.

Other survivor benefits are available depending on the age and relationship of the survivors. The following persons may be eligible and should contact the Social Security Administration to apply.

1. Surviving spouse age 60 or older, or if disabled then 50
2. Surviving spouse under 60 who cares for dependent children under age 16 or disabled adult children
3. Children of the deceased person under age 18 or disabled
4. Dependent parents age 62 or older

The best way to apply is to visit the SSA website and complete the online questionnaire at **www.ssa.gov**. The author has found the SSA website to be one of the best-designed and most helpful government websites. Be sure to review the website and print out relevant checklists prior to visiting the local Social Security office.

What survivor benefits are available for deceased federal employees and veterans?

If the deceased person was a federal employee or retiree, or was receiving benefits as the survivor of a federal retiree, you will need to notify the appropriate department to stop the benefit payment. There are countless benefit programs which may be affected by the death, so describing them here is near impossible. The best approach is to monitor the deceased person's checking accounts for any government deposits. You should be able to determine the source of the deposit from the monthly statement or by asking the financial institution to review it. After learning the source, you can search the Internet for more information about this type of benefit and then begin making some phone calls.

As a general matter, you should contact the Office of Personnel Management to inform the office about the deceased person's death. You may obtain the appropriate forms by calling (888) 767-6738 or submit the form online at **www.opm.gov/retire**.

Benefit payments received after the date of death must be returned. If a paper check was issued, then it should be returned to the address it came from along with a note stating the date of death. If the deposit occurred electronically, then inform the financial institution and request it return the money.

If you know the deceased person received any benefit through the Department of Veterans' Affairs, try contacting the Survivor Services department. The author has found this department to be very effective at providing counsel in this area. **www.vba.va.gov/survivors**

Federal employees who qualify for retirement benefits are registered under either the Civil Service Retirement System or the Federal Employees Retirement System. Also see this helpful non-government website: **http://federalretirement.net**.

What survivor benefits are available for deceased persons enrolled in the Arizona State Retirement System?

Survivors of current and former state employees enrolled in the Arizona State Retirement System will have benefits to apply for. The first step is to request a Survivor Benefits packet by calling (800) 621-3778 or by visiting a local office. You will need the deceased person's name, date of death, and social security number to proceed. When you file the documentation, you may be asked for proof of authority from the probate court depending on how the beneficiary was designated. The beneficiaries are usually entitled to two times the contributions made by a non-retired member (or higher in some cases) or for retired members, an amount equal to the contributions made prior to retirement less benefits already paid. There are several annuity options, which can be made by the beneficiaries, if the deceased person was still working, or by the deceased person, if retired. Further information about survivor benefits is available from the ASRS website.
https://www.azasrs.gov/content/pdf/fact_sheets/Survivor_Benefits.pdf

What survivor benefits are available through the deceased person's private employer?

If the deceased person was employed at time of death, be sure to contact the employer to determine whether the deceased person had any life, health, or accident insurance. The deceased person may also be due a final paycheck for wages, vacation, or sick leave.

In some cases, you may also find evidence of a retirement account with a former employer. Sometimes the survivors discover an unknown retirement account when the employer sends a tax reporting form in January of the year after death.   It may be worth a proactive effort to contact the former employer if you suspect the deceased person left a retirement account there.

If the deceased person belonged to a union or professional organization, check to see if they offer a death benefit for their members.

What type of notice should I give to the apartment manager where the deceased person lived?

If the deceased person was renting an apartment or house, then notify the landlord or property manager of the death and ask for a copy of the lease. After you have reviewed the terms of the lease, you should speak with the landlord or manager about the procedure for ending the lease. You will want to inquire whether the estate will be responsible for the balance of the lease term if the property is vacated promptly and left in good condition. Also, you should inquire about the status of the security deposit, if any.

DETERMINE WHETHER PROBATE IS NEEDED

As mentioned early in this chapter, the objective during this stage of administration is to compile enough information about the deceased person's assets and liabilities to determine what type of estate administration will be needed. This determination depends on how the assets are titled, whether there are beneficiary designations, the value of the assets (both aggregate and separate), and where they are located. Without primary source information, it is difficult to begin the estate administration process, let alone complete it.

Depending on the personality and organizational habits of the deceased person, the process of gathering information may be very simple.   The deceased person may have left you with a file folder, notebook, or document that contains all – or at least most – of the information you need. If the deceased person retained an estate attorney to prepare an estate plan, the attorney may have some of this information ready for you.

What if the deceased person failed to leave an updated list of assets?

If you cannot find a list of assets to start with, you should begin by monitoring the deceased person's mail. Bank statements can tell most of the story. You should also seek access to financial information on the deceased person's computer or online. If you manage to gain access to a financial software program or to the deceased person's online banking profile, you may find a goldmine of information to help you.

Other resources include the deceased person's accountant, or if none, prior year tax returns that you can find. Evidence of investment accounts may lead you to a financial advisor.

You should collect real estate deeds, mortgage information, loan documents, life insurance policies, annuity contracts, retirement savings statements, car titles – in other words, look for the most recent data about anything related to the deceased person's finances.

Estate settlement is similar to solving a jigsaw puzzle. Each piece must fit somewhere, and the puzzle would not be complete without any one of them. Unfortunately, sometimes it is hard to determine whether you have all of the puzzle pieces. You will have to do the best you can and then determine the legal steps necessary to administer the estate.

When should I retain an estate attorney?

Once you have obtained the bulk of information you need to identify assets and liabilities, you may want to meet with an estate attorney. The initial purpose of retaining an attorney at this point is to determine the primary approach to administering the estate. The estate attorney can tell you whether a probate action is necessary, and if so, what kind of probate action. If there is a trust document, the attorney will help you understand the process of settling a trust. Perhaps the most important task for the attorney is to determine who has authority to administer the estate and help give that person written authority to act.

When is a probate action required in Arizona?

Under Arizona law, the general rule is that if the deceased person owned more than $100,000 of equity in real estate, or more than $75,000 of personal property (including physical possessions and money), then a probate action is required to transfer the assets to the heirs. *See ARS 14-3971 et. al.* However, there are numerous exceptions to this rule.

First, exclude any asset that is owned jointly with a surviving person and includes reference to "with right of survivorship" in its titling. Sometimes this is hard to determine. For real estate, you may have to order a copy of the current deed to the property (called a "vesting deed") in order to examine how the deed was written. For motor vehicles, you may need to obtain a copy of the title to see whether the title uses the "AND/OR" designation or the "OR" designation, which may determine whether a probate action is required.

Second, exclude assets held in a trust. Trust assets bypass probate because they belong to the trust, not to the estate. In some cases, it may be difficult to determine whether an asset was put into trust or not. For example, you may find a bank account held in the deceased person's personal name, but another document signed by the deceased person saying that the account has been assigned to the trust.

Third, exclude any assets with a designated beneficiary who survives the deceased person. Under Arizona law, the designation of a beneficiary may take several forms.

- *POD Designations.* Personal banking accounts may have designated beneficiaries. This is called a "pay on death designation" or "POD." Some financial institutions will use the designation "in trust for" or "ITF," which is treated the same as the POD designation. *See ARS 14-6201 et. al. and ARS 6-236.*
- *TOD Designations.* Personal investment accounts may also have designated beneficiaries. This is called a "transfer on death designation" or "TOD." *See ARS 14-6301 et. al.*
- *Beneficiary Deeds.* Real estate may be held subject to a beneficiary deed. The deed, which names one or more beneficiaries on it, is recorded in the county where the property is located. A title search may be needed to confirm the presence of the beneficiary deed. *See ARS 33-405.*
- *Beneficiary Designations.* Although typically used with non-probate assets such as retirement accounts and annuities, Arizona law seems to imply that other personal property interests such as stock in closely-held companies and membership interests in limited liability companies may be

transferred to named beneficiaries without a probate action. *See ARS 14-6101.*

However, a beneficiary designation is ineffective when the designated beneficiary is no longer living, or when drafted or recorded improperly.

After you have excluded all of the above-described assets from the determination, add up the total net values of the remaining real estate and personal property as of the date of death. If either category limit is exceeded, then a probate action will be necessary. However, if neither category limit is exceeded, then Arizona law provides several non-probate alternatives to transfer the assets out of the deceased person's name to the heirs or beneficiaries. These alternatives are referred to in the Arizona statutes as small estate affidavits, and by many attorneys and financial institutions as non-probate affidavits. They are intended to avoid most of the formalities associated with probate.

How is the value of real estate determined for this purpose?

When determining whether a probate action is needed for real estate, an appraisal of fair market value is unnecessary. Under Arizona law, the amount of equity is calculated by using the current year's assessed value for property tax purposes less any outstanding debt. *See ARS 14-3971(E)(1).* Specifically, the statute refers to the "full cash value of the property as shown on the assessment rolls for the year in which the decedent died." This amount is sometimes substantially different than the fair market value. For example, the fair market value may be $250,000, but the assessed value for property tax purposes only $195,000.

How is the value of personal property determined for this purpose?

If the value of real property is less than $100,000, then the necessity of a probate action depends on the value of the personal property. This process is relatively simple provided you can access date of death values for the money accounts. However, you also have to calculate the value of the deceased person's tangible personal property, also known as stuff. For this task you have some flexibility. In general, a deceased person's clothing, household furnishings, and other personal effects can be valued loosely. These are items of emotional value which are often worth much more to the deceased person than anyone else. They are commonly donated to charity, piled in the trash, or distributed to family members as mementos of their loved one.

On the other hand, many people who die will have left some things capable of being sold to the general public. Some of these items may need to be appraised. Examples include bicycles, stamp collections, coin collections, gold, diamond rings, computers, golf clubs, firearms, automobiles, and motorcycles. You should be able to estimate the value of many tangible personal property items with a little research on the Internet or by phone. Other items, such as a stamp collection, will require taking the item to an appraiser for an expert's review. Many collector items are worth far less than the owner might have hoped, but it is your responsibility to find out.

In general, you can use informal appraisals whenever possible. However, there are exceptions. First, you should obtain formal appraisals if there are beneficiaries who are likely to dispute the amount or form of their inheritance. Second, you will need a formal appraisal if the deceased person's estate must file an estate tax return.

What if the deceased person had a living trust?

Many people choose to establish revocable living trusts ("living trusts") as the primary component of an estate plan. The process of administering the trust of someone who died is called trust settlement.

A living trust can provide a handful of benefits, but its primary purpose is usually to avoid the necessity of a probate action. In fact, a living trust achieves its purpose very effectively when all property otherwise subject to probate is re-titled into the name of the living trust prior to the death of the property owner. It may help to think of a living trust like a candy bowl. The candy pieces represent the various assets placed into the trust. After the death of the original owner, the entire bowl is given to a successor trustee, or manager, who is responsible for managing the distribution of the candy. A probate action is not required to distribute the candy because the pieces are not owned personally by the transferor. From the perspective of the candy, the candy belonged to the bowl – not the original owner – at the time of the death. The original owner's death does not affect the ownership of the candy. Thus, no probate action is required.

Although a living trust is intended to avoid the necessity of a probate action, the existence of a living trust does not guarantee the absence of a probate after a death. Some assets subject to probate may have been omitted from the living trust by accident or intention. If there is no surviving owner or beneficiary, these assets can only be transferred by probate action or small estate affidavit. Even in the most carefully planned estate, the proceeds from a wrongful death lawsuit or insurance settlement could trigger a probate action if paid to the estate of the deceased person. Thus, it is possible for an estate administration to include both a probate action and trust settlement.

How do I proceed if there is no living trust and the estate does not require probate?

If the deceased person did not have a living trust and you have also determined that a probate action is not required, then you may proceed to administer the estate informally. The typical tasks might include preparation of a small estate affidavit, removal of the deceased owner's name from jointly owned assets and transfer of assets to the named beneficiaries. Although simple in most cases, the process of administering an estate informally can be very complicated and time consuming. For example, there may be complex income tax issues when transferring an annuity or retirement account.

If you are the estate administrator, your tasks may include identifying the proper beneficiaries of each asset and making sure they actually receive it. Even with the benefit of non-probate alternatives, you may still find the estate administration process to be confusing and frustrating. The small estate affidavits are more complicated than you might anticipate and they may require substantial costs to implement.

The estate administrator is still responsible for handling the various government benefits, wrapping up annuities, applying for life insurance death benefits, and arranging for transfer of retirement accounts. Real estate may have to be sold, if none of the beneficiaries want to keep it. And of course, a final income tax return and maybe even a fiduciary income tax return could be required. Estate settlement in Arizona can be burdensome even without a probate action.

What if a financial institution demands to see "Letters Testamentary" before releasing any information?

Be aware that many well-intentioned employees at financial institutions and government agencies will unknowingly lead you astray. For example, an employee at a financial institution may follow a procedural checklist and ask for Letters Testamentary or something similar. They are referring to a document issued by a court as a result of filing a probate. However, you may already know that a probate is unnecessary and become frustrated by the request. Do not be alarmed – this is a common problem. Many first level customer service agents are not trained to understand estate laws. Larger companies are usually aware that small estate affidavits are available in Arizona, but its customer service agents may not have state-specific interpretations available for quick reference.

If you know a small estate affidavit is sufficient, you may have to familiarize the agent with the Arizona law. A suggested follow-up approach is to submit the correct documents – not the Letters – and include a copy of the relevant Arizona statute so the company's attorneys can review it. The author is aware of a few situations where a company required a probate action, even though not required by Arizona law. The most common culprit is a title company asked to insure a real estate transaction, but this is rare.

A word about dealing with financial institutions is appropriate here. You should anticipate interacting with employees of financial institutions who know less than you do about estate administration. This may surprise you, but see it as an opportunity. If you sound confident, but remain courteous and patient, you can accomplish much. For example, when you call an investment company regarding a deceased person's brokerage account, individual retirement account, or annuity, do not assume that the customer service agent you speak with knows exactly how to proceed. The agent's instinct will be to give an answer – any answer – even when the agent does not know the answer. Often the agent will refer to a cheat sheet from a computer to determine how to respond. As a practical matter, the initial reply will be, "Please send a death certificate and a copy of the Letters Testamentary." The first request is reasonable, but not always necessary; while the second request is commonly incorrect. In many cases no probate is required, so requesting Letters of Personal Representative from a probate court does not make sense. A small estate affidavit may be sufficient to close the account. In other cases, the presentation of relevant pages from a living trust document is adequate. Be careful not to assume that because an account is owned by a living trust, the customer service agent will understand how this type of account is transferred after death.

For many companies and agencies, you may need to find the specific department that deals with "survivor services" or something to that effect. If there is such a department, they are usually very helpful and will save you time and effort.

A wise approach is to create an easily accessible file with common information that financial institutions and other companies will ask for. The file should include the tax identification number for the estate (if any), the deceased person's final address, date of birth, social security number, date of death, and mother's maiden name.

Chapter 3

Create Fiduciary Authority

When a probate action is required or if the deceased person had a living trust, you will need evidence of your authority to act on behalf of the estate or trust. This authority – referred to here as fiduciary authority – will be granted by a probate court or by the living trust document itself. A fiduciary is any person who looks after the assets of another whose assets they are in charge of. In this case you will be appointed as fiduciary to protect the interests of the heirs or beneficiaries. This is known as a fiduciary duty. When you agree to administer an estate or living trust, you will need documentation to declare acceptance of your fiduciary duty before you are permitted to take control of the deceased person's assets.

HOW TO OPEN A PROBATE

How do I know if a will is valid?

It usually is not that difficult to identify whether a will document is valid. A will is usually labeled as such on the first page. It is a written document, signed and dated by the will maker, and usually by witnesses. The more difficult tasks may be to identify whether you are in possession of the most recent will and to find the original will as opposed to a copy.

A proper will is (1) handwritten or printed on paper, (2) signed by the will maker, and (3) signed by at least two adult witnesses, each of whom signed within a reasonable time after that person witnessed either the signing of the will or the will maker's acknowledgement that he or she signed the will. *See ARS 14-2502(A).*

It is permissible for someone to direct another person to sign the will, provided the person making the will is present, conscious, and directs the other person to sign it on his or her behalf. *See ARS 14-2502(A)(2).*

A will can be made self-proved if the will maker and the witnesses sign in the presence of a notary public. This means that you will not have to submit affidavits by witnesses or others who can identify the will maker's handwriting in order to prove that the signature is genuine. *See ARS 14-2504(B).*

Each witness must be generally competent to sign as a witness, but need not be a disinterested witness. In other words, the spouse or child of the person making the will is an eligible witness. This might not be the best practice, but Arizona law specifically permits it. *See ARS 14-2505.*

Arizona law also permits the use of holographic wills. A holographic will is a document intended to be a will that fails to comply with the proper execution requirements. Most holographic wills are simple, informal and handwritten. Others may have the will maker's signature on a pre-printed will form, but lack the necessary witnesses. For a holographic will to be admitted to probate, its material provisions must be in the handwriting of the deceased person, and the document must be signed. The holographic will need not be witnessed or notarized. What provisions qualify as material is open for debate, but they logically would include the appointment of a personal representative and a description of who should inherit the property. Other provisions need not be handwritten, although it is hard to imagine someone typing up a will themselves, and then handwriting certain important provisions. In other words, a holographic will that is entirely typewritten and signed by the deceased person is not valid because its material provisions are not in the handwriting of the deceased person. *See ARS 14-2503 and ARS 14-2502(B).*

What if the original will cannot be found?

In general, a probate court will not admit a will unless the registrar has examined the original. However, you may still submit a copy of a will if you have strong evidence to prove that the copy you have is valid and the original although lost, still exists. *See ARS 14-3415.* You will have to prove by a "preponderance of the evidence" that the submitted copy is a true copy of the original. This is not easy. You will have to include the testimony of at least one credible witness that the copy is a true copy, although it is not necessary that this witness be an attesting witness to the will. For example, the lawyer who drafted the will may not have signed as a witness, but could provide the testimony. The testimony of a witness is likely insufficient if the probate court finds that the will was last seen in the possession of the deceased person. In this case it will be presumed that the deceased person revoked the will.

Although it is difficult to imagine the following scenario, what if the probate court finds that a will was validly signed, not revoked, but no copies are ever found. In this case, the court might still reproduce the contents of the will based on the "clear and convincing evidence" brought to the probate court's attention. *See ARS 14-3415(C).*

May a will include a separate list of things to give to people?

Many people create a written list to state who they want to receive specific items after death. The list is rarely intended as a will by itself, although if there is no will, then it may be treated as a holographic will. The list is treated as an exhibit to the will. It may be created before or after the signing of the will and be valid. If you find more than one list and they both refer to the same property, the more recently signed list controls. *See ARS 14-2513.*

What if the will was drafted in another state?

A will does not have to be drafted and signed in Arizona to be admitted to probate in Arizona. Provided the will met the requirements for a valid will in the state it was prepared, then it will be admissible in Arizona. Further, the other state's law will apply to any controversy surrounding the effect of a provision in the will unless the law is contrary to the requirements relating to exempt property and family allowances or is contrary to Arizona public policy.

What if the deceased person did not leave a will?

If no one can find a valid will signed by the deceased person, then you will have to proceed without one. If a probate action is necessary, Arizona probate law will determine who may be appointed to serve as personal representative.

Under Arizona law, there are limitations regarding who may apply for appointment as personal representative. *See ARS 14-3301.* As a practical matter, the proposed personal representative will be the person who files the application. If there is no will, *ARS 14-3203* prescribes the following order of priority to determine who may be appointed as personal representative:

1. Surviving spouse who is also a devisee of the deceased person
2. Other devisees of the deceased person
3. Surviving spouse
4. Other heirs of the deceased person
5. Department of Veterans Services if deceased person was a veteran
6. Any creditor of the deceased person, after 45 days
7. Public fiduciary

An objection to an appointment can be made only in formal proceedings. Thus, if someone does object to the informal appointment, the case must be converted to a formal probate.

What is the difference between formal and informal probate?

The probate process in any state is challenging to understand, but with the right approach, not that difficult in Arizona. Most probate actions in Arizona are "informal," which means they are completed with minimal court supervision. No visits to a court building are necessary and there will not be a judge overseeing your every move. A small number of probate actions are "formal," which involve stricter notice requirements, court hearings and increased supervision. For example, a formal probate action is required when the court must intervene to resolve a dispute between interested parties.

Absent a dispute, you can likely proceed with an informal probate. Although an informal probate is simpler than a formal probate, the process is characterized by unusual, intricate terminology and requirements that often do not make sense to anyone who works outside the probate court. The difficulty level is increased by the fact that you are solely responsible for learning what you do not know. Staff members at the probate court have no obligation to help you beyond explaining basic filing requirements. However, armed with enough knowledge, resources, and determination, it is possible to complete an informal probate action from start to finish without an attorney.

Probate is a complicated process with confusing terminology. Although many people successfully maneuver through the process without professional assistance, you can save a lot of time and frustration by consulting with an estate attorney before proceeding. The process will be overwhelming if you have never been involved with an Arizona probate before. In recent years the Arizona state legislature has attempted to streamline the rules among the various counties, but critical differences in procedure still exist. An attorney in the county where you file the probate should know these unique procedural requirements and help you complete the filing requirements without any trouble.

The situation is much more challenging when a formal probate is required. Formal probates are reserved for cases when there is question or controversy regarding the validity of the will, choice of personal representative, identification of heirs, or an asset requires increased court supervision. *See ARS 14-3401 et. al. and ARS 14-3501 et. al.* If you suspect a formal probate is required, then retain an estate attorney who accepts formal cases to assist you. A small portion of estate attorneys specialize in handling contested probate matters.

Where do I file for appointment as personal representative?

You should file the application in the county where the deceased person was domiciled at the time of death. *See ARS 14-3201.* The place of domicile refers to the primary residence. If this is not clear, you will have to examine other factors such as voting registration to determine the place of domicile.

If the deceased person was not living in Arizona, you should file in the county where the property is located.

What is the process for opening a probate?

Typically the person responsible for administering the estate will file an application with the probate court for informal appointment of personal representative in the deceased person's county of residence. If the person had a will, the person is said to have died testate. In a testate estate, the application involves two primary tasks. First, the probate registrar will examine the original will that you submit in order to recommend that the probate court certify its validity. Second, the court will issue Letters of Personal Representative to the willing person or persons nominated in the will.

If there is no valid will, the application will nominate a person or persons with priority for appointment under Arizona law to serve as personal representative. A person who dies without a valid will is said to have died intestate.

Although the Arizona state legislature has attempted to make the application process consistent across the state, each county will have some unique requirements.

In general, the initial filing must include the original will, if any, and a substantial set of court documents. They include:

- Application for Informal Probate of Will and Appointment of Personal Representative (testate) or Application for Informal Appointment of Personal Representative (intestate)
- Probate Information Form
- Certificate of Completion of Non-Licensed Fiduciary and Personal Representative Training Programs
- Acceptance of the Duties of Personal Representative
- Statement of Informal Probate of Will and Appointment of Personal Representative (testate) or Statement of Appointment of Personal Representative (intestate)
- Order to Personal Representative and Acknowledgement and Information to Heirs/Devisees
- Letters of Personal Representative

The initial set of documents should also include a waiver for any person who has priority to serve as personal representative in the will, but decides not to serve. In addition, the application must include a bond for the proposed personal representative unless the will or all of the heirs waive the bond requirement.

How do I complete the training programs to become a Personal Representative?

In 2012 the Arizona Supreme Court adopted new rules requiring non-licensed fiduciaries to complete two training programs prior to appointment as personal representative. One program deals with fiduciary duties in general, and the other explains the duties of a personal representative. Both training modules are offered as Power Point-style presentations. They are available at **www.azcourts.gov/probate/Training.aspx**.

What do I receive back from the probate court when it approves the application?

When the application is submitted, the objective is to obtain a certified copy of the Letters of Personal Representative back from the probate court. The name of this document is confusing because the word "letter" is not used in its normal sense. This is a good example of what makes probate confusing. You would think the document might be called "Proof of Authority" or "Confirmation of Appointment," but the probate courts continue to use the traditional – perhaps antiquated – term "letters."

Absent extraordinary circumstances, the document will probably only consist of one sentence. For example, "John Smith has been appointed and is authorized to act as Personal Representative of the Estate without restriction." The letters do not actually appoint the personal representative, but rather authorize the appointed personal representative to act. The document is the evidence of authority for the personal representative to act on behalf of the estate; i.e., it is the prize received for submitting a satisfactory petition. A certified copy of the letters must then be presented to the appropriate individuals and financial institutions in order to collect or transfer assets of the estate. The cost of a certified copy may vary by county, but is approximately $27 plus $0.50 per page in the document.

Can we open the probate before obtaining a death certificate?

Yes. There is no requirement that you obtain a death certificate before filing an application to open probate. You may file the application as soon as five days have passed after the deceased person's death. It may take a few weeks before you receive any certified copies of the death certificate. The head start does allow you to take care of some things. For example, you can open a bank account in the name of the estate, although you probably will not be able to close out or transfer other accounts until you can provide a death certificate.

What is a Demand for Notice?

In some cases, a person, company or organization will file a Demand for Notice with the court before or after the filing of a probate application. The purpose of this filing is to protect the interests of an interested party. For example, if the deceased person received benefits from the Arizona Long Term Care System (ALTCS), then notice must be given to ALTCS prior to the application. This gives ALTCS, or its collection division, the opportunity to enforce its rights against the estate. The notice period must be at least 14 days. A waiver of notice may be obtained in order to avoid the notice period. *See ARS 14-3204.*

How much does a typical probate cost?

The initial application fee for an informal probate varies by county, but is approximately $200 to $250 including various court costs and filing fees. There is also a fee for each certified copy of the letters.

You may be able to obtain basic self-help forms from the probate court's website, a law library, or the local bar association.

A formal probate may include additional costs for notices and service of process. After the letters are issued, the personal representative will need to publish a Notice to Creditors in a local newspaper. The cost may vary widely depending on the current newspaper advertising rates. Also, there may be a cost to obtain appraisals of hard-to-value assets.

In Arizona, an estate attorney will usually agree to handle an uncontested, informal probate from start to finish for about $2,000 to $5,000. The majority of law firms use hourly rates to calculate the fee, but an increasing number are switching to fixed fee pricing structures. A formal probate will be much more expensive. Hourly rates are used to calculate the fee because the amount of legal work involved is hard to predict at the beginning.

What is a bond requirement?

By default a personal representative must obtain a bond to insure against loss or theft of estate assets. The bond is purchased from an insurance company with an amount at least equal to the personal representative's best estimate of the value of the probate assets and one year's income. A company specializing in bonds may be used for this purpose, however, most major property insurance companies (e.g., State Farm, Allstate) also sell this type of bond.

The vast majority of wills waive the standard bond requirement because of the expense. If the will does not waive the bond or there was no will, then a bond is generally required. However, if there is no valid will, all of the heirs may waive the bond requirement in writing. Likewise, if a valid will fails to waive the bond, all of the named beneficiaries may still choose to waive the bond requirement in writing. The waiver must be unanimous. *See ARS 14-3603.*

When bond is required, the personal representative will need to secure it before the court will issue certified letters.

What if I can't qualify for the full bond amount?

If you cannot qualify for a bond based on the full value of the estate plus one year's income, the informal probate process cannot be used. The probate registrar will not reduce the required bond amount unless the letters contain a restriction of certain assets by the court. *See ARS 14-3604(A).* If qualifying for the full bond amount is a problem, then you have two options. First, you can waive your right to serve as personal representative and let someone else do it. Second, you can petition for formal probate and request that some of the assets be restricted so that they cannot be sold or distributed without prior court approval. This will reduce the required bond amount.

What are the steps of a typical probate?

In general, every probate follows a consistent chronological order. Here is an abridged version of the steps involved in any probate:

Step One: Initiate Probate and Appoint Personal Representative
1. Submit application with bond or waivers of bond
2. Receive Letters of Personal Representative

Step Two: Notify Heirs, Devisees, and Creditors
1. Send notices to each heir and devisee
2. Notify known creditors
3. Publish notice to unknown creditors

Step Three: Inventory the Estate
1. Prepare inventory of all estate assets
2. Re-title each asset into name of estate

Step Four: Pay Claims
1. Pay valid debts
2. Send out notices of disallowance (if necessary)

Step Five: Distribute the Estate
1. Determine who the beneficiaries are
2. Transfer assets to beneficiaries using appropriate method

Step Six: Close the Estate
1. Prepare final accounting or waivers of accounting
2. File closing statement

PROBATE NOTICE REQUIREMENTS

Who is entitled to receive a copy of the will?

The first order of business for a personal representative is to open a checking account for the estate and begin to pay bills. However, you should not tarry with meeting the notice requirements under Arizona law. Once proper notice is received, the heir has only four months to contest the probate. It is a good practice to start this clock as soon as possible.

Within 30 days after appointment, the personal representative must deliver a copy of the following documents to all devisees, heirs, and other interested persons. *See ARS 14-3705 and 14-3306(B).*

1. Notice of Informal Probate and Appointment of Personal Representative
2. Order to Personal Representative and Acknowledgement and Information to Heirs/Devisees
3. The probated will, if applicable

A devisee is someone named in the will as a beneficiary. An heir is someone who would inherit the deceased person's property assuming there is no will. The required documents must be delivered or sent by first class mail to each heir and devisee whose address is reasonably available to the personal representative. The personal representative must also file the original Notice of Informal Probate and Appointment of Personal Representative with the court within 45 days after appointment, along with a Proof of Mailing for the Notice and the Order.

What about notice to creditors?

Unless the personal representative was appointed more than two years after the deceased person's date of death, the personal representative must publish a notice once a week for three consecutive weeks in a newspaper published generally in the county where the probate was opened. *See ARS 14-3801.* The notice is intended to inform unknown creditors that they have four months after the date of the first publication to present their claims to the personal representative. A similar notice must be sent directly to all known creditors of the estate. This may include mortgage lenders, health care providers, and credit card companies.

Can I keep information about the assets private and away from people who need not have it?

Within 90 days after appointment, the personal representative must prepare a detailed inventory of the estate assets including their fair market values as of the deceased person's death. *See ARS 14-3706.* In some cases the personal representative may want to prevent certain people from seeing a copy of the inventory. Any person with a financial interest in the estate must be given a copy upon request, but the inventory is private in regards to everyone else. The two filing options are:

1. *Private Option*: No copy is sent to the probate court, but instead the personal representative sends copies to (a) each of the heirs if the deceased person died intestate (without a will) or to each of the devisees (named beneficiaries) if a will was admitted to probate; and (b) to any other interested person who requests a copy of the inventory.

> 2. *Public Option*: A copy is sent to the probate court. Additional copies are sent to each interested party that requests a copy, if any.

At first glance, the private option seems better if confidentiality is preferred. However, a recent rule change was made to better preserve the confidential nature of the inventory at the probate court. Under Rule 7 of the Arizona Rules of Probate Procedure, the inventory is a confidential document that is no longer maintained in the public record of a probate case. As a protected document, the general public has very limited access to the document. A person would have to obtain authorization from the probate court after showing good cause for needing a copy of the document.

Will a "no contest clause" prevent a disgruntled heir from contesting the probate?

Under Arizona law, a provision that attempts to penalize an interested person from contesting a probate is unenforceable if probable cause exists for that action. *See ARS 14-2517.* In other words, anyone can try to contest a probate, although the "no contest provision" will require the person to convince the court that the contest is legitimate.

Can the validity of the will be challenged after it is admitted to probate?

Yes, any heir or interested party may contest the validity of a will unless more than four months have passed since that person received notice. The most common challenges to a will are based on lack of testamentary capacity and undue influence.

Arizona law presumes a person who signs a will has the requisite mental capacity to do so. *See Estate of Thomas, 105, Ariz. 186, 189, 461 P.2d 484, 487 (1969).* In fact, it is very difficult to prove otherwise. In order to establish capacity, the signer must understand the following at the time of execution:

- The nature of the act he or she is doing;
- The nature and/or character of his or her property; and
- The natural heirs of his or her bounty.

See Estate of O'Connor, 74 Ariz. 248, 259, 246 P.2d 1063, 1070 (1952).

Since the determinative test is based on capacity at the time of signing, it is almost impossible to prove incapacity after the fact. It is even possible for a person diagnosed as mentally incapacitated by a physician to have the requisite capacity to sign a will – if the signer exhibits an adequate understanding of its provisions and a clear desire to sign it.

The more likely challenge to succeed is a claim of undue influence. The person making the contest must prove by clear and convincing evidence that the will was procured by undue influence. The test is whether a person uses his power over the mind of the deceased to make the latter's desires conform to his own so that the will does not conform to the wishes of the signer but to those of the person exercising the undue influence. *See Evans v. Liston, 116 Ariz. 218, 568 P.2d 1116.* The probate court will use several factors to weigh the existence of undue influence. These factors include:

- Whether a person had made any fraudulent representations to the deceased;
- Whether the will was hastily executed;
- Whether the execution of the will was concealed;
- Whether the person who benefitted was active in securing the drafting and execution of the will;
- Whether the will was consistent with prior declarations of the signer;
- Whether the provisions were reasonable rather than unnatural in view of the signer's attitude, views and family;
- Whether the signer was susceptible to undue influence;
- Whether there existed a confidential relationship between the signer and the person allegedly exerting the undue influence.

A will is less susceptible to challenge if prepared under the supervision of an estate attorney and the process to do so was initiated, paid for, and directed at all times by the deceased person. An estate attorney is most likely to follow an established system for communicating with the client, determining capacity, and exercising a consistent approach to the signing and witnessing of a will. However, even these formalities are still no guarantee that a disgruntled heir will not challenge a will – and perhaps even succeed.

HOW TO BEGIN TRUST SETTLEMENT

What is the process for administering a living trust?

A trust is managed by a trustee. The creator of a living trust usually, but not always, serves as trustee for the trust during his or her lifetime. After the death of the person who created the trust, the first step is to appoint a new trustee. A successor trustee is usually designated in the trust document. If the living trust was established by a married couple, the surviving spouse may be appointed as the sole trustee. However, the trust document may also appoint two or more persons to serve as co-trustees.

Under Arizona law, a designated trustee does not have to serve as trustee if he or she prefers not to. *See ARS 14-10701.* There is no public reward for serving as trustee. It is a challenging and generally thankless job, which requires a substantial amount of time. A trustee can also expect some grief from other family members, even when it is least expected. If a designated trustee declines to serve, that person should sign a waiver document. The procedure for declining to serve and finding the next successor trustee is usually described in the trust document.

On the other hand, if a designated trustee desires to serve, then that person should sign a document evidencing the person's acceptance of the duties. When combined with an updated Certification of Trust, this is how the trustee will prove his or her authority to act on behalf of the trust. Technically, the same person could also accept the duties by simply acting; i.e., by accepting delivery of the trust property into the trustee's name or performing trustee duties. *See ARS 14-10701(A)(2).* The only exception occurs when the trustee begins doing something right away that is necessary to preserve trust property, but then notifies a beneficiary within a reasonable time that he or she does not want to continue serving as trustee. *See ARS 14-10701(C).*

No bond is required unless a probate court finds that a bond is needed or the trust document requires it. A bond requirement is rare for a trustee because it is assumed that a person creating a trust would appoint a trustworthy person as trustee.

What is a Certification of Trust?

Every trust should be accompanied by a Certification of Trust. This is a document with essential information about the trust that can be shared publicly. It will name the current trustee, and whether the trust is revocable or irrevocable, and the tax identification number for the trust, and the powers of the trustee. The information that must be included in a Certification of Trust is described in *ARS 14-11013*. When a formerly revocable living trust becomes irrevocable after the death of its creator, the successor trustee should prepare a new Certification of Trust.

Can two people serve as trustee together?

Yes, there is nothing that legally prevents two or more persons from acting together as trustee. A co-trustee is supposed to participate in all trustee decisions unless he or she is unable to do so because of absence, illness, disqualification, or other temporary incapacity. *See ARS 14-10703(C).* A co-trustee may also delegate his or her duties to another person, provided the document does not prohibit this. *See ARS 14-10703(D).*

If three co-trustees are unable to reach a unanimous decision about something, a majority of the co-trustees may act on behalf of the trust. *See ARS 14-10703(A).* The dissenting co-trustee would be protected from liability for such action. *See ARS 14-10703(F).*

What if there are no trustees named in the document who are willing and able to serve as trustee?

If there is no one willing and able to serve as trustee, the trust document might include a provision that gives someone the power to appoint a successor trustee. That person should find someone willing to serve as trustee and document the appointment in writing, along with the acceptance of duties. *See ARS 14-10704(C)(1).*

Absent such a provision in the trust document, the qualified beneficiaries (a term that includes both current and contingent trust beneficiaries) may, by unanimous consent, appoint any qualified person or company as successor trustee. *See ARS 14-10704(C)(2).* If this is not possible, then the probate court may appoint a successor trustee upon petition and a hearing. *See ARS 14-10704(C)(3).*

What if the acting trustee wants to resign?

A trustee would typically resign by giving 30 days notice to the qualified beneficiaries and any co-trustees. *See ARS 14-10705(A).* This procedure may vary depending on specific provisions in the trust document.

What if the beneficiaries want to remove a trustee?

A prudent trustee will consider what protections are in place to prevent a disgruntled beneficiary from removing the trustee.

The answer initially depends on the terms of the trust document itself. Trust documents drafted by estate attorneys will usually outline a procedure for removal of a trustee. Many will include a provision that gives an independent person or a majority of beneficiaries the right to remove a trustee.

In addition, a co-trustee or beneficiary may always petition the probate court to remove a trustee. Under Arizona law, the petitioner must prove one of the following to be true. *See ARS 14-10706.*

1. The trustee has committed a material breach of trust.
2. There is a lack of cooperation among co-trustees that substantially impairs the administration of the trust.
3. The trustee is unfit, unwilling, or failing to act for the benefit of the beneficiaries.
4. There has been a substantial change of circumstances and removal is requested by all of the qualified beneficiaries; and a removal is not inconsistent with a material purpose of the trust.

How much compensation does a trustee receive?

Under Arizona law, a trustee is entitled to compensation that is reasonable under the circumstances. *See ARS 14-10708.* It can be difficult to say what is reasonable. If a trustee wants to take compensation, one measurement to start with would be to take the trustee's hourly wage from regular employment and multiply that by the number of hours he or she performed trustee duties. Provided the hourly wage is reasonable – perhaps $25 to $75/hour – no one is likely to challenge the amount. A second measurement might be to examine what a trust company or certified fiduciary would charge because, unless the trustee is an estate attorney or certified fiduciary, the trustee's fee should be less than that.

The trust document itself may answer the question. Some trusts will include a method to determine the compensation. Unless the compensation specified by the terms of the document is unreasonably low or high, the amount should be respected if reviewed by a court.

On the other hand, the trustee need not take compensation and could simply get reimbursed for expenses. *See ARS 14-10709.* In fact, most family member trustees choose not to do so out of respect for the deceased family member. This does not mean a trustee must decline compensation, but a trustee should be aware that any compensation is treated as taxable income to the trustee.

What is a trust protector?

You may find a provision for a trust protector in the trust document. The trust protector has specific powers described in the trust document, which often include the power to (1) remove and appoint a trustee, (2) modify or amend the trust document to achieve favorable tax status, or (3) change the applicable state law, among other powers. *See ARS 14-10818.* The trust protector is not a trustee. Usually the named trust protector will be an independent person such as an attorney or accountant.

TRUST BENEFICIARY NOTICE REQUIREMENTS

What information must a trustee disclose to trust beneficiaries?

Under Arizona law a trustee has a duty to inform and report to the beneficiaries of the trust. *See ARS 14-10813.* The duty to inform includes an initial requirement to notify the beneficiaries within 60 days after a formerly revocable trust becomes irrevocable (usually after the trust creator's death) or within 60 days after the trustee accepts the duties of trusteeship. The duty to report includes an annual requirement to deliver a trustee's report to current beneficiaries.

The trustee also has a general duty to keep the qualified beneficiaries reasonably informed about the administration of the trust and of the material facts necessary for the beneficiaries to protect their interests. The definition of "qualified beneficiary" includes both current beneficiaries, and the contingent beneficiaries who would inherit if a current beneficiary died or the trust was dissolved.

There are two exceptions to this general duty. First, the trust document might include a statement to the opposite effect, instructing the trustee, to the extent permitted by law, to refrain from distributing information about the trust to the beneficiaries. Second, the trustee may decide that a beneficiary's request for information is unreasonable under the circumstances.

However, not all information may be withheld. Regardless of what the trust document says about the subject, the trustee must provide a copy of the portions of the trust document that are necessary to describe the beneficiary's interest to any beneficiary who makes the request. In addition, the trustee must provide a trustee's report to current beneficiaries, and other beneficiaries who request it, at least annually. *See ARS 14-10813(B) and ARS 14-10813(C).* This report serves to provide a minimum amount of essential information about the trust to the beneficiaries. Arizona law does not permit the creation of a secret trust fund for a beneficiary.

In addition, all current beneficiaries, plus any contingent beneficiaries who request it, must be provided with a trustee's report each year. The report must identify the trust property, liabilities, receipts and disbursements, including the source and amount of the trustee's compensation. There is no statutory form for this report, although it should be detailed enough to satisfy the curiosity of a reasonable beneficiary.

The notices may be delivered by first class mail, personal delivery, delivery to last known place of residence, or by e-mail if the address is valid. *See ARS 14-10109(A).* Notices are not required for a beneficiary who cannot be located by the trustee after reasonable effort.

What information must be on the initial Notice to Trust Beneficiaries?

The trustee must deliver an initial trust beneficiary notification to all qualified beneficiaries of the trust. The notice must (1) state the trustee's name and contact information; (2) disclose the beneficiary's right to request a copy of the portions of the trust document that are necessary to describe the beneficiary's interest (generally, a copy of the entire document); and (3) disclose the beneficiary's right to receive or request a trustee's report at least annually. *See ARS 14-10813(B)(3).*

What about a Notice to Creditors?

A trustee is not required to publish a notice to creditors in a newspaper. However, the property of the trust is subject to the claims of the deceased person's creditors, costs of a probate administration, and the funeral or cremation expenses. *See ARS 14-10505(A)(3).* Thus, all known creditors of the estate should be notified even if no probate action is required. A claim will be barred if not presented to the trustee within the time prescribed in the written notice. *See ARS 14-6103(B).*

In the absence of written notice, the deceased person's creditors will be barred from presenting claims when two years have passed since the deceased person's death. *See ARS 14-3803(A).* If concerned about unknown creditors, the trustee might choose to publish a notice to creditors in a newspaper similar to the notice required in a probate action. *See ARS 14-6103(A).* This will reduce the time unknown creditors have to present claims from two years to four months after first publication.

Can anyone contest the validity of a trust?

Yes. Any interested person may contest the validity of a trust, provided they do it within the time prescribed by law. The common challenges – lack of capacity and undue influence – are the same as for a challenge to a will. A person may contest the validity of a trust within the earlier of (1) one year after the trust creator's death, or (2) four months after the trustee sent the required notice described in *ARS 14-10813. See ARS 14-10604(A).* This rule emphasizes the benefit to the trustee of sending out the required beneficiary notices as soon as possible.

As trustee, you may proceed to distribute the trust property before the expiration of the four month period. Even if the trust is later determined to be invalid, the trustee is not liable for making distributions unless either (1) the trustee has actual knowledge of a pending contest, or (2) someone has notified the trustee of a possible contest and proceeded to begin the contest within 60 days. *See ARS 14-10604(B).* If the trust is declared invalid, then the beneficiaries are liable to return the distributions they received. *See ARS 14-10604(C).*

TAX NOTICE REQUIREMENTS

Do I need to apply for a tax ID number?

Yes, most likely, in order to report any income earned by the estate or trust after the deceased person's date of death. The person responsible for administering the estate will need to apply for a taxpayer identification number (aka employer identification number). The number is provided to financial institutions that need it to process transactions and report income to the estate. A financial institution will ask for the estate's tax ID number prior to opening an account in the name of the estate.

Similarly, if a living trust is used to administer the estate, the trustee may need to apply for a taxpayer identification number on behalf of the trust.

What do I send to the IRS?

If there is a surviving spouse, he or she can file a final joint federal income tax return. If not, then the person designated as personal representative is responsible for filing the final return.

If you need a copy of the deceased person's prior year federal income tax return, you can order a copy by filling out two forms:

1. Form 56: Notice Concerning Fiduciary Relationship
2. Form 4506: Request for a Copy of Tax Return

An accountant usually submits these forms, although anyone can obtain them by visiting the IRS website at **www.irs.gov** or by calling (800) 829-3676.

What do I send to the Arizona Department of Revenue?

The estate will also have to file a final Arizona income tax return if the deceased person's adjusted gross income was higher than $5,500 ($11,000 if married). *See ARS 43-301.*

If you need a copy of the deceased person's prior year income tax return, you can submit a request to receive it by filling out two forms:

1. Form 210: Notice of Assumption of Fiduciary Duties
2. Form 450: Request for Certified Copies of Document

These forms are available on the Department of Revenue website at **www.azdor.gov** or by calling (602) 542-4260.

How do I get a tax release?

The estate may need to obtain a certificate from the Arizona Department of Revenue showing that no income tax is due. *See ARS 43-1361.* This is often required in formal probates, but also recommended for any other estate settlement when the assets are substantial, or if you just want to be extra cautious. Technically, the tax release certificate should be filed with the court at the same time as the final accounting. Arizona law requires a certificate if all of the following are true:

1. The estate is subject to probate.
2. The value of the estate exceeds $20,000 at time of death.
3. The estate has a beneficiary that is not an Arizona resident.

If needed, the personal representative should request the tax release certificate when filing the final income tax return for the estate. The certificate request should be mailed to: Arizona Department of Revenue, 1600 W. Monroe, Room 610, Phoenix, AZ 85007. The department must be in possession of Form 210 to issue the certificate. Also, upon request by the department, the personal representative must submit a copy of the will or trust document when the estate's gross income is $5,000 or more. Call (602) 716-7809 for further assistance.

What tax returns are due for the estate?

If the estate or trust earns income after the date of death, the estate or trust may need to file Form 1041 with the IRS and Form 141AZ with the Arizona Department of Revenue. These forms are only required if the estate or trust has any taxable income. The Arizona form is required prior to issuance of a tax release certificate, even if there is no income to report. Contact an accountant familiar with preparation of fiduciary tax returns in order to meet these filing requirements.

What estate taxes are due?

Commonly referred to as the death tax, the purpose of the estate tax is to prevent family dynasties from securing the lion's share of our nation's wealth. The estate tax is not a tax on wealth, but rather a tax on the transfer of wealth from a deceased person to heirs. Similarly, it should not be referred to as an inheritance tax because the tax is paid by the deceased person's estate before the heirs receive any inheritance.

The federal estate tax rate is 18 to 40%, with the maximum rate applicable to *taxable* transfers above $1,000,000. However, a transfer is not taxable to the extent it is exempt. Many states have their own version of the estate tax, although Arizona does not. The Arizona estate tax was repealed in 2002. The author is unaware of any efforts by the state legislature to re-enact the estate tax.

Who is exempt from the estate tax?

For persons dying in 2016, up to $5.45 million may be transferred free of tax using the applicable estate tax exemption. The exemption is unified with the gift tax because the exemption amount is reduced by the total amount of taxable gifts made during the deceased person's lifetime. Thus, lifetime gifts of $1 million would reduce the applicable estate tax exemption to $4.45 million. The exemption amount adjusts annually for inflation.

The estate tax laws are subject to the political winds of change. It is hard to predict what Congress may do as future Presidents come and go from office. There are regular discussions about changing the credit amount or repealing the estate tax altogether, but any action requires broad agreement in Congress. In today's political climate, the chances of broad agreement about repealing the estate tax are slim. Most likely the estate tax is here to stay, with adjustments made to the exemption amount and tax rates from time to time.

Chapter 4

Identify the Beneficiaries

When determining who will receive the deceased person's assets, the principal rule is that titling always controls. In other words, the key is to examine how the asset is held. For example, was it owned by the deceased person alone? Was it owned together with a spouse and/or child? Or was the property held in a trust? The answer to the titling question will determine the appropriate transfer method.

REAL ESTATE

How do I verify the ownership of real estate?

It perhaps goes without saying, but one cannot verify the titling of real estate without examining the current recorded deed. In some cases, a review of several deeds, affidavits, and death certificates may be necessary in order to make sense of the current ownership.

The first place to look is the county assessor's website where the property is located. You should have no trouble finding the website using any popular Internet search engine. Look for a link to property records and then use the search procedures to find the property. Many counties, but not all, also provide free access to images of the recorded deed going back many years. If not, then you might have to contact a title company and request a search for the deed. Your estate attorney should be able to do this too.

The county assessor website is the best place to start because it will show how the assessor believes the property is titled. It is not always reliable, because the information may be out of date and sometimes there are data entry errors, but it certainly can verify what you already believe to be true. After you have studied how the property is held, then you can determine what steps you must take to transfer the property.

What if the property is held in the deceased person's name alone?

When there is only one owner of a property, the deed will usually say something like:

John Williams, an unmarried man

or

John Williams, as his sole and separate property

If you find the deceased person to be the sole owner of a property, then a probate action is likely necessary to transfer ownership. This is the classic probate scenario, although a small estate affidavit may work as an alternative.

When you hear the word "probate," the next question will be whether the deceased person had a valid will. If yes, the terms of the will should describe who inherits the property. In some cases, the property may be part of a specific bequest. For example, the will might say, "I give my primary residence to my daughter, Jennifer Williams, outright free of trust." Absent a specific bequest, the residuary or default language will apply. Of course, the residuary language could say almost anything, so the exact text of the will must be carefully read and interpreted to identify the beneficiary.

What if the property is held by a trust?

If you find the property is held in the name of a living trust, the deed will usually say something like:

John Williams, as Trustee of the Williams Family Living Trust

When a property is held in a living trust, a probate action will not be needed. In fact, the successor trustee can proceed rather quickly to sell the property or distribute it to a beneficiary identified in the trust agreement. Similar to a will, the trust document may refer to the property in a specific bequest or include it in the residuary language.

What if the deed refers to a surviving spouse?

Listed in the order you are most likely to see them in Arizona, here are examples of what the deed might say if the property is jointly owned with a surviving spouse:

> John Williams and Susan Williams, as community property with right of survivorship
>
> John Williams and Susan Williams, as joint tenants with right of survivorship
>
> John Williams and Susan Williams, husband and wife
>
> John Williams and Susan Williams, as community property

There are a few other variations you might see, such as when the husband and wife own an unequal share (e.g. 60%/40%) and joint tenancy without right of survivorship, but these are much less common.

Arizona is one of nine community property law states. In summary, community property means that both husband and wife own an undivided one-half (50%) interest in the property. For property titled as community property with right of survivorship, the surviving spouse automatically inherits the deceased spouse's one-half interest. No probate action is required.

For property held as joint tenants with right of survivorship, the result is the same. The only difference is related to the income tax (to be addressed later). Joint tenancy titling is available to anyone – not just married couples. So it is possible that a deed includes the names of a husband, wife, and child. If husband is survived by wife and child, then wife and child will continue to own the property as joint tenants with right of survivorship.

If the property is held as "husband and wife" or as "community property" but without right of survivorship, there is a possibility that the surviving spouse will not inherit the deceased spouse's one-half interest. Without the "right of survivorship" feature, the deceased spouse's one-half interest must be distributed to whoever is named in the will. If there is no will, then Arizona intestacy law will determine who receives the one-half interest.

This situation is often unexpected and can lead to odd results. No one wants to hear that a probate action is required simply because the words "with right of survivorship" were not added to the titling of the deed. On the other hand, this may be precisely what the deceased person intended. Especially in a second marriage situation, for example, a husband might prefer his share go to someone else besides his wife – probably his children from a prior marriage. If that is the case, the husband's will document should clarify this. But if there is no will, Arizona law directs one-half to the surviving spouse and splits the other one-half among the husband's children. The end result is that the property would be owned 75% by the surviving spouse and 25% by her stepchildren.

The toughest situation is when the property is titled "husband and wife" but the deceased spouse had no intention of leaving the property to anyone but the surviving spouse. The deceased spouse's one-half is subject to probate in order to transfer the property solely to the spouse. A small estate affidavit might be used to avoid the probate action, but this is still an expensive step that could otherwise have been avoided.

What if the deed refers to a spouse who is deceased?

You may find the property titled in the name of the deceased person and a predeceased spouse. This occurs commonly because often no one bothers to update the property records after the first spouse's death. However, it is entirely possible that a death certificate for the prior deceased spouse was recorded long ago, and that might not be evident without a title search.

If the property is titled as community property with right of survivorship or joint tenancy with right of survivorship, then you should make sure death certificates for both husband and wife are recorded and then proceed to probate the property.

If the property is titled without right of survivorship (e.g., husband and wife), then you should request a title search to determine whether anything was recorded at the first spouse's death. If not, you will have to resolve this issue before the property can be transferred or sold. You will probably have to use a probate action or small estate affidavit to account for the one-half interest of the first spouse to die before you can probate the interest of the second spouse to die. This can be quite difficult, especially if it has been many years since the first spouse died.

What if the property is held in joint tenancy with a child?

If both a deceased spouse and a surviving child are named on the deed as joint tenants with right of survivorship, the property belongs to the surviving child. However, this choice of property titling has its disadvantages and is thus relatively unusual.

Assuming the deed clearly states that the property is held as "joint tenants with right of survivorship," the surviving child will inherit the property. If there are multiple children named on the deed, they will inherit the property and the right of survivorship feature will continue in effect for them.

What if the property is owned by a limited liability company?

If you find the property is owned by a limited liability company ("LLC"), then you will have to dig deeper to find out who inherits the property.

You might also find the property is owned in the name of an S-corporation, partnership, or even sometimes, a C-corporation. For various reasons, these are unpopular entities for holding real estate, but the way of handling them is basically the same for all business entities.

It is very common for investment properties, both inside and outside the state of Arizona, to be held in the name of a LLC. This is a popular way to achieve some asset protection for the owner. The intent is to isolate the property from other assets in the event of a lawsuit or business failure relating to that property.

You will need to determine who the owners of the LLC are. In Arizona, the owners are called members. You can find information about the members of an Arizona LLC at the Arizona Corporation Commission website. **www.cc.state.az.us**

Although this search will usually give you the answer you need, it might not if you learn the member is another entity, or if there are multiple members. If the LLC is a business entity with multiple members, it is likely to have a separate operating agreement that might include specific provisions for how to allocate the membership interests of a deceased member. You must obtain a copy of the operating agreement to find out. If the members never signed an operating agreement, or if it does not include such a provision, you will have to assume that the deceased person's interest is subject to probate.

For most LLCs, you will find that the member is the deceased person or the deceased person and a surviving spouse. In the latter case, the same rules for joint spousal ownership of real property apply here. For example, the members might own their interest as community property with right of survivorship. *See ARS 29-732.01.*

Notwithstanding the above, Arizona law seems to imply that membership interests in an LLC may be transferred to designated beneficiaries without a probate action. *See ARS 14-6101.* Whether this is permitted by the statute or not is debatable, but you might find a beneficiary designation with the corporate documents.

It is also common to find that a LLC is owned by the deceased person's living trust. This means that a probate action is not needed and the beneficiary can be determined by reviewing the trust document.

If the property is subject to probate, does that mean a probate action is the only option?

No. In Arizona, the owner of real property may record a separate deed supplementing the deed of ownership, which designates a beneficiary in the event of the owner's death. *See ARS 33-405.* If properly recorded and the named beneficiary is living, then a probate is unnecessary. If there are multiple owners of the property, the deed becomes effective upon the death of the last surviving owner.

The deed is specific to the property it describes, so if you know the deceased person owned multiple properties, then you might look for multiple beneficiary deeds.

A beneficiary deed may designate a single beneficiary or multiple beneficiaries using any type of joint ownership permitted in Arizona. The deed may even designate successor beneficiaries if a primary beneficiary is deceased. You will need to review the actual text of the deed to know for sure.

A beneficiary deed is only effective if it was recorded in the county where the property is located. It may be revoked, but a revocation would have to be recorded similar to the deed itself.

Beneficiary deeds are becoming more common in Arizona. They are also well-suited to avoid probate of timeshare interests deeded in Arizona.

BANK AND INVESTMENT ACCOUNTS

How do I verify the ownership of money accounts?

Personal banking accounts, along with taxable investments (not retirement accounts) such as certificates of deposit, mutual funds, and stocks, have similar ownership designations as real estate. Some of the terminology is different, but the titling always controls. The first step is to examine the caption of a monthly or quarterly statement. Typically, the name on the account is reproduced exactly on each statement. For example, if you see "John Williams and Susan Williams, JTWROS" above the mailing address, then you know the account is owned by John and Susan as joint tenants with right of survivorship.

Arizona law treats banking accounts differently than taxable investment accounts. Monies in deposit in a checking account, savings account, certificate of deposit, and a credit union share account are all subject to *ARS 14-6204*, which describes the types of accounts available.

What if the account is titled in the deceased person's name alone?

If the account is in the deceased person's name alone, the account is likely subject to probate. *See ARS 14-6212(C).* This is another example of a classic probate scenario, although a pay-on-death ("POD") designation may eliminate the need for a probate action if the designated beneficiary is living.

Unless the account is specifically allocated to someone in a will, the account is likely to be liquidated and distributed as part of a residuary allocation to the beneficiaries during probate.

What if the account is owned jointly with someone else?

Arizona law refers to joint accounts as multiple party accounts. When a multiple party account is opened, the owners have the option of including a right of survivorship feature. If this option is selected, then the surviving joint owner (or owners) is entitled to the account, regardless of any conflicting provisions in the deceased account owner's will. No probate action is necessary.

In the event there is no surviving joint owner, the account is subject to probate. However, the account may have a pay-on-death ("POD") designation, which eliminates the need for probate.

If the right of survivorship option is not selected, then the funds in the account continue to be available to the surviving joint owner or owners (at least in a practical sense). However, the deceased owner's portion of the account is subject to probate. In order to legally remove the deceased owner's name from the account, a probate action is required. *See ARS 14-6212(C).*

It is another matter – and often a difficult one – to determine what portion of the account belongs to the deceased person. Technically, the account belongs to the joint owners in proportion to the amount they each deposited to the account, less expenditures. For married couples, the allocation is presumed to be equal.

As a practical matter, this situation is unusual. In the vast majority of cases, the joint owners would select the right of survivorship feature. Thus, the account belongs entirely to the surviving owner. *See ARS 14-6212(A).*

In the event there is no surviving joint owner, the account is subject to probate. The pay-on-death ("POD") designation is not available for multiple party accounts when the right of survivorship option is not selected. *See ARS 14-6212(C).*

What is a pay-on-death designation?

Single party accounts with right of survivorship may include a pay-on-death ("POD") designation, which means the bank or credit union will have a record of the designated beneficiary for the account. If there is one named beneficiary, and that beneficiary is alive, then the funds in the account belong to the named beneficiary upon filing of a death certificate. If there are multiple beneficiaries, then the funds in the account belong to the named beneficiaries in equal amounts. If there are no surviving named beneficiaries, then the POD designation is disregarded and the funds in the account belong to the estate of the deceased owner; i.e., subject to probate.

However, if the account is a multiple party account with a right of survivorship, then the funds in the account belong to the surviving owner or owners. The POD designation continues in effect, but would not be carried out until the death of the last surviving owner. *See ARS 14-6212(B).*

For example, Mom owned a Certificate of Deposit at Chase Bank. Although she was the sole owner, she had designated her two children as POD beneficiaries using a pre-printed form provided to her by the bank. Since a POD designation overrides any conflicting provision in Mom's will, the two children acquire ownership rights to the account immediately upon Mom's death. Under *ARS 14-6214(B)(2)*, the account is payable to the two children in equal shares. If one of them is deceased, the entire account is payable to the surviving child. If both are deceased, the account is subject to probate.

May an investment account have a pay-on-death designation?

Yes. An investment account may have a pay-on-death ("POD") designation, although it is properly described as a transfer-on-death ("TOD") designation. *See ARS 14-6301 et. al.* When reviewing the accounts of a deceased person, be careful to note the type of investment account. A regular, non-retirement investment account may have a TOD designation, but a retirement account or annuity cannot. The latter types of accounts, including life insurance accounts, are subject to beneficiary designations, which can be more complex to interpret.

The TOD designation works just like the POD designation. If a deceased person is sole owner of an account with a TOD designation, the named beneficiary in the TOD designation is entitled to the funds in the account. If there is no surviving beneficiary named in the TOD designation, then the account is subject to probate. For multiple party accounts, the TOD designation is not carried out until the death of the last surviving owner.

The terms pay-on-death and transfer-on-death may be used interchangeably by financial institutions and the general public. There are few differences between them.

What is an ITF designation?

Some financial institutions may use the term "in trust for" (ITF) to describe the same concept as pay-on-death or transfer-on-death.

What if a surviving person is named as power of attorney on the account?

The owner of a bank or credit union account may name another person as agent under a durable power of attorney to manage the account. When the financial institution agrees to honor the terms of the durable power of attorney, it will often include the name of the agent in the title of the account. Both owner and agent have full control and access, although the agent owes a fiduciary duty to the owner. In the context of estate administration, the power of attorney is irrelevant because it must expire upon the death of the owner.

On the other hand, it is worth noting that many bank and credit union employees will fail to realize that a durable power of attorney is no longer valid after the account owner's death. If the person administering the estate is different than the person named as agent in the durable power of attorney, the administrator should notify the financial institution about the death as soon as possible and remove the power of attorney designation from the account.

Alternatively, the account owner may have designated someone as agent for the account, also known as an agency designation. This means that a person other than the account owner may make transactions on behalf of the owner. *See ARS 14-6224.* Similar to an agent designated by durable power of attorney, the agency designation is useful for basic incapacity planning, so the agent could manage the account even if the owner becomes incapacitated. The agent does not have any ownership rights to the account, with the exception that it is possible for the agent to also be named as pay-on-death beneficiary and inherit the account upon the death of the owner.

The agency designation expires at the death of the last remaining owner who appointed the agent. In other words, if you are the agent, you will no longer be able to make account transactions after the death of the last remaining owner. Of course, this may only be temporary until you gain access to the account by other means.

What if the account is owned by a living trust?

Any bank or credit union account may be owned by a living trust, provided the financial institution permits it. By its nature, a living trust survives after the death of the person or persons who created it, so the trust document controls the disposition of an account owned by the living trust. The successor trustee reviews the terms of the trust document to determine whether to transfer the account to a trust beneficiary. The only immediate changes might be to inform the financial institution of a change in trustee and provide a new taxpayer ID number for the trust. After the financial institution is satisfied with proof of the new trustee's authority, the trustee may proceed to manage the account on behalf of the trust beneficiaries.

LIFE INSURANCE, ANNUITIES, AND RETIREMENT ACCOUNTS

Who is entitled to receive the death benefits?

As a general rule, life insurance policies, annuities, and retirement accounts owned by a deceased person are not subject to probate because they are subject to the terms of a beneficiary designation. The designated beneficiary is entitled to receive the available funds in the account upon the owner's death. However, if there are no surviving beneficiaries named in the beneficiary designation, the account may be subject to probate. The result may depend on whether the account agreement has a default beneficiary designation.

For example, Dad is the owner and insured person on a life insurance policy. Dad named Son as the sole beneficiary on a written beneficiary designation. Son dies before Dad. Upon Dad's subsequent death, the fine print of the life insurance policy might state that if the named beneficiary is deceased, then the death benefit is payable to the Dad's heirs-at-law. Thus, if Dad is survived by Daughter, then Daughter receives the proceeds without a probate action.

For each account that may be subject to a beneficiary designation, your task is to verify whether a beneficiary designation is in effect and identify the beneficiaries. You are off to a good start if you can locate an account or policy application with the deceased person's important records. The application is likely to include a section regarding the initial beneficiary designation. The application also may include a preprinted summary description of the default beneficiary designation method. At times the account or policy owner will make changes to the beneficiary designation prior to death, so you must still verify the current beneficiary designation with the financial institution after you have authority to do so.

This process can take some time, especially because the financial institution is likely to request a death certificate before it will release information of this nature.

What if the beneficiary designation conflicts with the deceased person's will?

A beneficiary designation will override conflicting provisions in a will. For example, if a deceased person's will names all three children as beneficiaries, but the beneficiary designation for an account only names one of them, the other two children are not entitled to any portion of the account.

What if a trust is named as beneficiary?

It is relatively common for the owner of a life insurance policy or annuity to name a living trust as beneficiary. Upon the death of the owner, the life insurance company will pay the death benefit to the named successor trustee. If the named trust is to be established by will after the death of the owner, the trustee should prepare a Certification of Trust and obtain a taxpayer ID number as soon as possible.

A retirement account may also be paid to a trust. This may be done for a variety of estate planning reasons.

CARS, RVs, AND MOBILE HOMES

How do I verify the ownership of a motor vehicle?

The Motor Vehicle Division of the Arizona Department of Transportation issues titles for automobiles, recreational vehicles, and mobile homes not affixed to the land. These titles are evidence of ownership and are the basis for determining who will inherit the asset upon the death of an owner. There is no public registry of title information, so you will have to find the title for one of these assets in the deceased person's possessions.

If a deceased person owned a motor vehicle that was financed or leased, it is highly unlikely that the deceased person even had possession of the title. You will need to find the original purchase or lease agreement to learn how the car was titled initially. The proof of registration in the car is another source of information, although not necessarily adequate to fully describe how title was held. If you find nothing, you will need to contact the company who is financing or leasing the vehicle in order to report the death and determine the chain of ownership.

When searching for ownership information, you might think it possible to order a duplicate title from the Motor Vehicle Division. Unfortunately, their procedure is to send the duplicate title directly to the lien holder on record so that may not help you. If you can present a lien release document or power of attorney from the lien holder, then you could order the duplicate title. This might work if the lien was paid off prior to the deceased person's death. If you believe the lien was paid in full, but you cannot find the title, or a lien release, then you should request a new copy of the lien release from the lien holder. This may require examining the deceased person's banking history to see who the deceased person had been making payments to.

Also, if the deceased person had a driver license, it is good practice to inform the Motor Vehicle Division of the death.

What if the title is registered in the deceased person's name alone?

The first line of the caption on a title will describe how the motor vehicle is owned. The title to a mobile home will look exactly the same, although this discussion refers to motor vehicles. If the deceased person's name is the only name on the title, then the motor vehicle is likely subject to probate. However, the motor vehicle may qualify for transfer of ownership using a small estate affidavit (referred to by the MVD as a non-probate affidavit) available directly from the Motor Vehicle Division.

There is also another relatively unknown method to avoid a probate action. In Arizona, the sole owner of a motor vehicle may designate a beneficiary similar to a pay-on-death designation for a bank account or a beneficiary deed for real estate. *See Form 96-0561 "Beneficiary Designation"* available on the MVD website. **http://mvd.azdot.gov**. If stapled to and presented with the current title, the beneficiary designation is effective for title transfer after death. *See ARS 28-2055(B).* Assuming this condition is met, the beneficiary may apply for a new title in the beneficiary's name upon presentation of a death certificate.

Although the beneficiary designation form refers to motor vehicles, Arizona law permits the Motor Vehicle Division to accept beneficiary designations for mobile homes. *See ARS 28-2063(B) and ARS 28-2055(B).*

What if the deceased person is listed as joint owner with another person?

The Motor Vehicle Division of the Arizona Department of Transportation permits three types of joint ownership on motor vehicle and mobile home titles. Presumably they are intended to simplify the choices available, but they can be rather difficult to tell apart. The types of joint ownership are as follows:

1. *"John Williams or Susan Williams"* – This form of ownership is commonly used by auto dealerships when they sell a motor vehicle to a married couple. During the owners' joint lifetimes, either owner is authorized to transfer the vehicle. Upon the death of a joint owner, the surviving owner does not need to update the title because it is assumed that either owner has full authority to transfer the vehicle. Upon the death of the remaining owner, the vehicle is subject to probate.

2. *"John Williams and Susan Williams"* – This form of ownership is less common. During the owners' joint lifetimes, the signature of both owners is required to transfer the vehicle. Upon the

death of either joint owner, the interest of the deceased owner is subject to probate.

3. *"John Williams and/or Susan Williams"* – This form of ownership is better described as joint tenancy with right of survivorship. During the owners' joint lifetimes, the signature of both owners is required to transfer the vehicle. Upon the death of a joint owner, the surviving owner does not need to update the title because of the right of survivorship, although a death certificate would be needed to transfer the vehicle. Upon the death of the remaining owner, the vehicle is subject to probate.

From an estate planning perspective, many joint owners would choose the AND/OR designation to prevent unauthorized transfers during lifetime. However, auto dealerships regularly suggest the OR designation because it provides the most flexibility.

The Motor Vehicle Division does not permit use of a beneficiary designation when the title is held by more than one person. Although no action is required by a surviving owner, he or she might choose to reapply for title in order to add a beneficiary designation and avoid probate.

WHO INHERITS THE PROBATE ASSETS?

A substantial portion of this book describes how assets can be transferred to a surviving owner or beneficiary without the need for a probate action. However, you may find that a probate action is still necessary to transfer some or all of a deceased person's assets. The personal representative appointed by the court will then need to determine who is entitled to inherit the probate assets.

Who inherits under the will?

If the deceased person left a valid will that is admissible to a probate court, then the personal representative should proceed to follow its direction when allocating inheritance. In some cases the personal representative may not be certain how to interpret a specific provision, especially if it was written by the deceased person or by someone unfamiliar with the intricacies of estate law. When this occurs the personal representative should request an opinion from an estate attorney. If the dollar amount at issue is substantial, the attorney may recommend a hearing at the probate court so it can issue a ruling on the matter.

In many cases there is no reason to open a probate and thus, the will is never submitted to the probate court. Assuming the named personal representative believes the will to be valid, the personal representative must still abide by the provisions of the will to determine who inherits what. For example, if a small estate affidavit is used to transfer a motor vehicle, Arizona law requires the person submitting the affidavit to state under oath that he or she is the successor to the motor vehicle (under the terms of the will).

Who inherits when the deceased person failed to leave a valid will?

If the deceased person did not have a will, this is referred to as dying intestate. Arizona law carefully prescribes the rules to determine the beneficiaries in this case. The following is a highly simplified summary of the Arizona intestacy laws. *See ARS 14-2102 and ARS 14-2103.* The actual rules are more complex in order to address very unusual situations, but this summary will cover the vast majority of cases.

Surviving spouse, no descendants
- Surviving spouse is the sole heir

Surviving spouse, all descendants belong to spouse and deceased
- Surviving spouse is the sole heir

Surviving spouse, one or more descendants not related to spouse
- Surviving spouse inherits one-half of deceased person's separate property, if any; and
- Descendants of deceased person inherit one-half of deceased person's separate property and all of deceased person's one-half of the community property

Unmarried, with descendants
- Children of deceased person inherit equally
- Share of a deceased child is distributed to the surviving children of the deceased child

Unmarried, no descendants
- Parents of deceased person inherit equally, or all to surviving parent
- If both parents are deceased, then to the descendants of the deceased person's parents (i.e., brothers and sisters) in equal shares

The term "descendants" refers to a deceased person's children and descendants of the children. *See ARS 14-1201(11).* Biological and adopted children are included, but stepchildren are not. *See ARS 14-1201(5).* The term "community property" refers to the joint assets of a married couple, as opposed to the separate property of each spouse. *See ARS 14-1201(7).*

What does "to issue by representation" mean?

The will may include a provision leaving property to someone's issue by representation. The term "issue" refers to the person's descendants; i.e., children and grandchildren. Biological and adopted children are included, but stepchildren are not. *See ARS 14-1201(5).* The term "by representation" refers to the manner of allocating property among the descendants.

As a practical matter, a division by representation means equal distribution among the surviving children. Arizona intestacy laws use *by representation* by default, so it is commonly used in wills drafted by Arizona estate attorneys. *See ARS 14-2103.* However, another common survivorship provision is *per stirpes* which is effectively the same unless one or more children have predeceased.

In order to show the difference between the two options, assume Parent had two children who both predeceased Parent. Child 1 has one surviving child and Child 2 has three surviving children. If the will divides the property by representation, then all four grandchildren will receive an equal amount. But if the will divides the property *per stirpes*, then the surviving child of Child 1 will receive one-half and the three children of Child 2 will each receive one-sixth.

What if a family member died in the same accident as the deceased person?

In order to qualify as an heir under the Arizona intestacy laws, a person must survive at least five days after the death of the person whose property is subject to probate. Absent clear and convincing evidence that this is true, the heir is presumed to have predeceased. *See ARS 14-2104.*

What if a known child was not mentioned in the will?

If a parent fails to update a will after the birth of a child, Arizona law automatically includes the child as an heir. *See ARS 14-2302(A).* One exception would be if the parent clearly stated in the will that future children would be omitted as heirs. However, even a clear statement of this nature may be disregarded as it was when the will of Michael Jackson was probated.

A similar situation occurs when a parent fails to update a will after the birth of an additional child. Perhaps the will refers to two children, but the parent had a third child after the signing of the will. Arizona law automatically includes the third child unless an exception applies: (1) if it appears from the will that the omission was intentional, (2) the omitted child was provided for by non-probate transfer (e.g., life insurance) and there is evidence that the parent intended this result. *See ARS 14-3202(A) and ARS 14-3202(D).* Absent an exception, the third child will inherit an interest equivalent to the other two children. *See ARS 14-2302(B).*

What if a potential heir has not been born yet?

If an heir is deceased, but the heir's wife or partner is pregnant with the heir's child, the child in gestation qualifies as an heir under the intestacy laws if the child lives at least five days after birth. *See ARS 14-2108.*

Perhaps a more interesting issue occurs when a deceased heir intentionally or unintentionally left frozen embryos or sperm for possible later fertilization. Arizona case law continues to abide by the underlying statute, which narrowly defines gestation. This would exclude a person who later – at least arguably – becomes an heir of the deceased person after artificial insemination and birth.

Are adopted children treated any differently than natural born children?

Unless the will says otherwise, adopted children are treated as children of the adopting parent and not of the natural parents. *See ARS 14-2705.*

What if the deceased person's will refers to a spouse but they are now separated or divorced?

Absent a marital agreement or court order saying otherwise, a final divorce decree severs the shared financial interests of a married couple for estate planning purposes. So if a deceased husband failed to update his will (or trust) after getting divorced, the wife is not an heir. *See ARS 14-2804.* On the other hand, a legal separation severs the community property interests of a married couple, but does not revoke a gift to a spouse in an estate plan.

What if an heir or beneficiary owed money to the deceased person?

A debt owed by an otherwise qualifying heir to the deceased person must be enforced if it was in writing. The deceased person's will or living trust might cancel the loan, but absent such a provision, the debt must be repaid to the estate. The personal representative is responsible for collecting on the debt. If appropriate, the amount of the outstanding debt can be deducted from the share payable to the heir.

What if a gift to an heir prior to the deceased person's death was actually meant as an advancement of inheritance?

The portion an heir would otherwise inherit could be reduced or eliminated if it can be shown that a lifetime gift was intended as a partial advancement of the heir's inheritance. In order for the gift to be treated as partial advancement, either the deceased person or the heir must have left a written declaration of intent to this effect. Of course, no scheming heir would ever let such a declaration be found, so the real question is whether anyone will find a declaration signed by the deceased person. *See ARS 14-2109.*

What if property specifically gifted to someone in the will was sold prior to death?

If property specifically identified in the will was sold by the deceased person prior to death, the gift – referred to as a specific devise – is effectively null and void. However, if the purchaser is still making payments on it, then the balance of the purchase price is payable to the beneficiary named in the will. *See ARS 14-2606(A)(4).*

It is another case if the property was sold or mortgaged by a person acting as agent for the owner prior to death. For example, if a deceased person's agent acting under a durable power of attorney sells the property, the beneficiary named in the will is entitled to a distribution amount equal to the net sale price or amount of the unpaid loan. *See ARS 14-2606(B).*

Does the signing of a new will invalidate an older list of things to distribute?

Many wills refer to a separate list for specifying who should receive various items of tangible personal property. The definition of tangible personal property includes clothing, collectibles, furniture, household goods, silverware, computers, sporting equipment, books, and the like. It does not include money gifts.

The personal representative should honor the terms of the list as long as it was signed or handwritten by the deceased person. The list is effective whether prepared before or after the will was signed, and can be changed after its initial creation. *See ARS 14-2513.*

If someone designated to receive an item on the list is deceased, the gift is canceled unless the terms of the will or list say otherwise.

Chapter 5

Creditor Issues

An important aspect of estate administration is handling of debts, expenses, and claims against the estate. As administrator for the estate you will want assurance that all of these items have been accounted for properly so you – and the beneficiaries – do not become personally responsible for them. When there is sufficient money to pay all debts, expenses, and claims, your job is relatively simple. The situation becomes much more challenging when there is not enough money to go around.

Sometimes a deceased person's estate will include one or more probate assets, but their value will not exceed the amount of outstanding debt. If the debts are substantial – and the creditors unforgiving – a personal representative may feel overwhelmed trying to sort things out. Provided the deceased person has some assets to speak of, the personal representative should consult with an estate attorney to determine the appropriate course of action.

What creditors have priority for payment?

If the deceased person's estate does not have enough money to pay all valid creditor claims in full, the personal representative will need to carefully prioritize the distribution of funds to the creditors. Under Arizona law, claims against the estate are prioritized as follows. *See ARS 14-3805.*

1. Expenses of administration (probate costs, personal representative compensation, attorney fees)
2. Funeral expenses
3. Federal taxes

4. Expenses of last illness (hospital, nursing home, etc.)
5. State taxes
6. All others

Any statutory allowances should be paid before the funeral expenses and other claims, but after the expenses of administration. In other words, the administration expenses are always the highest priority.

If there are multiple claims within a category and not enough funds left to pay them in full, the claims must be prorated according to their amounts.

If all the assets would be paid to creditors, can I just do nothing and hope they go away?

Yes, in theory, that might work. Creditors have two years after the debtor's date of death to present their claims. *See ARS 14-3803(A).* If none of the beneficiaries choose to petition for appointment as personal representative, and any other assets inherited from the deceased person are protected from creditors by law, then the beneficiaries could theoretically open a probate two years after the deceased person's death without having to deal with creditor issues.

The problem with this approach is that a creditor is allowed to petition a probate court to get appointed as personal representative, provided at least 45 days have passed since the date of death. For large debts, the creditor – or the creditor's debt collection agency – might be very willing to incur this expense and trouble for the possibility of collecting on the debt.

What debts is the estate responsible for?

The simple answer is that all valid claims must be paid. Of course, the personal representative might need to use some detective skills to smell out the bad claims. This is probably most likely to occur with medical billing. It can very difficult to know whether a medical bill is valid or not. But a personal representative has a duty to review any claims before they are paid.

If the personal representative believes a claim is not valid, the personal representative should mail a Notice of Disallowance to the prospective creditor. The creditor has 60 days after the mailing of the notice to file a petition for allowance with the probate court.

What debts are the survivors responsible for?

If the estate cannot pay all the valid debts of the deceased person, the pressing question is whether the surviving beneficiaries are responsible to pay them. The issues presented by this question are somewhat complicated when the deceased person was unmarried and very complicated when there is a surviving spouse.

If the deceased person was unmarried, no one else is responsible for payment of the debts. There are some important exceptions. If another person agreed in writing to be responsible for payment of the loan (i.e., a personal guarantee), then that person continues to be liable for the entire payment. The debt should be paid first out of any joint accounts that the deceased person shared with the other debtor, and if that is not sufficient, then the other debtor must pay out of his or her own funds.

For example, assume Dad set up a joint account with Son at a local credit union. At the same time Dad purchased a car and financed it. At Dad's death, he still owed $10,000 that the estate could not pay back. As long as Son never agreed to be responsible for the loan, he will not be responsible for paying it back. On the other hand, if Son purchased the car together with his Dad, and was a co-signer on the loan, then he will be responsible. Any money in the joint account at the credit union should be used first to pay off the loan.

If the deceased person was married, the answer is much more complicated. First, a summary of community property law is in order. Any asset acquired by either the husband or wife during the marriage is community property, except for property received by inheritance or gift. The latter items are separate property as long as they are segregated from the community property. Likewise, a community debt is a debt incurred during the marriage, provided the expense benefitted the family directly or was used to care for family property. A separate debt is a debt incurred prior to the marriage or any debt not incurred for the benefit of the family.

In order to explain, assume Husband and Wife get married. Husband had financed a purchase of investment property before the marriage. After marriage they changed the deed to community property with right of survivorship for estate planning purposes, but did not refinance the loan. Husband and Wife acquired additional community property during the marriage, and then Husband died. Provided Wife never agreed to pay Husband's pre-marital debt, Arizona law should prohibit a creditor collecting on the debt from Wife's share of the community property. The creditor may only collect from the Husband's share of the community property, along with Husband's separate assets. *See ARS 25-215(B).*

The problem here, of course, would be proving the investment property is community property. An aggressive plaintiff's attorney might argue the change of deed represented form over substance, or was fraudulent, and that all of the property should be available to the creditor.

At the death of a married person, all of the married couple's community property is subject to the claims for community debt, even if the surviving spouse did not approve of the deceased spouse's acquisition of the debt or was unaware of it. If the community property is insufficient to satisfy the claim, the separate property of the deceased person is available, if any. *See ARS 25-215(D).* The surviving spouse's separate property, if any, is not subject to the claims of the creditor unless he or she agreed to be liable for it.

For example, assume Husband committed a crime (before or during the marriage) and was ordered to pay restitution. This is a separate debt and certainly Wife's share of the community property should be protected.

Another interesting issue is when Husband incurs a community debt, but Wife was unaware or even disapproved. All of the community property is available to pay that debt, as long as the debt was money spent for the benefit of the family. For example, Husband goes out and finances a new car without Wife's approval (because she claims they can't afford it). She does not co-sign for the loan. The car is parked in the family garage and is used sometimes for family travel. If Husband died, all of their community property – including Wife's contribution to it – is exposed to that creditor. Only her separate property, if any, would not be exposed because she did not agree to pay the debt. *See ARS 25-215.*

In summary, if the debt is treated as a separate debt of the deceased spouse, then up to one-half of the community property (representing the deceased spouse's one-half) is available to pay the claim, along with the separate property of the deceased spouse. But if the debt is treated as a community debt, then all of the community property, and potentially even the separate property of both spouses, is available to pay the claim.

This discussion should make it clear how important it is for married couples to keep good records of what assets are classified as separate property. For couples who married young and/or did not have many assets prior to marriage, this is not really an issue. All of the property they acquire is community property, unless received by gift or inheritance. But for couples who marry when one or both spouses already own substantial assets, it can be very important to keep track of separate property – not just for a possible divorce settlement, but for determining what assets can be tapped to pay off creditors of the first spouse to die.

If an account is in a survivor's name alone, is it protected from the deceased person's creditors?

Not necessarily. In Arizona, the titling of the asset is not the only factor when determining whether the asset is treated as community or separate property. Imagine the common scenario where a husband purchases a car and puts the title in his name alone. The money used for the down payment and the ongoing payments comes out of community property earnings and savings. The car is community property.

If the estate is insolvent, can a creditor make a claim against other assets transferred outside probate?

Yes. A determined creditor can request payment from persons who inherited an asset outside the probate process. For example, if Child inherited an account from Dad through a pay-on-death designation at a bank, a creditor of Dad could demand payment from Child. In order to do so, the creditor would have to deliver a written demand to the personal representative. The personal representative may then request Child to give back up to the entire amount received from the bank account to the estate. If Child refuses, the personal representative (or the creditor itself) can initiate a court proceeding to obtain a judgment against Child. *See ARS 14-6102.* This process is subject to the two year statute of limitations against creditor claims. *See ARS 14-3803.*

Are any assets fully exempt from creditors?

Yes. Under Arizona law, up to $37,000 in statutory allowances is available to the family. These allowances take priority over all creditors except the expenses of administration. *See ARS 14-2401 et. al.*

Federal retirement plan accounts are exempt from creditors, with only one exception – if the deceased person owed back child support under *ARS 33-1126(D)*. In other words, the deceased person's 401k or 403b account may be transferred outside the reach of the deceased person's creditors. *See ARS 33-1126(B)*. Individual retirement arrangements ("IRAs") paid to Arizona beneficiaries are also exempt under state law, although there is a growing set of case law in other states that threatens to diminish the level of protection.

After the death of an insured person on a life insurance policy, the death benefit is protected from creditors in Arizona. The amount of the exemption is unlimited, provided the beneficiary did not also agree to be responsible for the debt. *See ARS 20-1131(A)*. However, Arizona law gives the surviving spouse and children up to $20,000 of claim-free life insurance proceeds even if they are also obligated to pay the debt. *See ARS 33-1126(A)(1)*. In other words, if a person dies with no assets, but owned a $20,000 life insurance policy, then the survivors can inherit the life insurance proceeds free of any creditor claims.

A surviving spouse may also qualify for a homestead exemption under Arizona law, which protects up to $150,000 of equity in a personal residence from creditors with some exceptions, including a mortgage, mechanic's lien, and child support. *See ARS 33-1101*. The homestead exemption is intended to prevent the attachment or forced sale of a personal residence to satisfy judgment creditors. In Arizona the exemption is automatic, which means that no special action is required to benefit from it, although a homestead declaration may be recorded if the homeowner has more than one eligible property. It should be noted that a determined creditor could force a sale of the home if there is more than $150,000 in equity. The spouse would keep the first $150,000, but the balance would be available to creditors.

What are statutory allowances?

The purpose of statutory allowances is to protect the welfare of a deceased person's spouse and dependent children. The underlying public policy is to make sure the family is not totally disinherited – by the deceased person or by creditors who wind up getting everything. Only the expenses of administration take priority over the statutory allowances. The available allowances are summarized here:

Homestead Allowance under ARS 14-2402
- $18,000 to the surviving spouse or dependent children

Family Allowance under ARS 14-2404 and 14-2405

- Up to $12,000 to the surviving spouse or dependent children

Exempt Property under ARS 14-2403
- Surviving spouse and children may take up to $7,000 worth of furniture, cars, furnishings, appliances, and personal effects.

Are assets held in a living trust exempt from creditors?

Similar rules apply when the deceased person had a living trust and probate is avoided. Under Arizona law, a living trust is subject to the claims of the deceased person's creditors, costs of administration of the estate, funeral expenses, and the statutory allowances to the extent the probate estate is inadequate to satisfy these claims. *See ARS 14-10505(A)(3).* In addition, a creditor can also seek payment from any persons who received inheritance through other non-probate transfers. *See ARS 14-6102.* Note that, like a will, the trust document itself may direct the source from which liabilities will be paid.

Will the State take the home when the deceased person was on Medicaid prior to death?

Medicaid is the federal program providing medical and long term nursing care to persons who cannot afford it. Although Medicaid is a federal program, each state administers its own version of the program. In Arizona, the state agency responsible for administering the program is the Arizona Health Care Cost Containment System ("AHCCCS"). Of particular concern in the context of estate administration, one of the programs that AHCCCS administers is the Arizona Long Term Care System ("ALTCS") for benefit of persons who cannot afford long term nursing care. For more information, visit the ALTCS program website at **www.ahcccs.state.az.us**.

Under ALTCS qualification rules, a person may be able to receive long term care benefits in a nursing home and retain a primary residence. Provided the applicant intends to return home, or is renting it out for income, the home is an "excluded resource" for determining whether the applicant qualifies for benefits.

A common Medicaid planning technique is to transfer the home to a spouse prior to applying. If the home is not owned by the spouse receiving ALTCS benefits, then the State cannot place a lien on the home. But if the applicant is unmarried, then the State can place a lien on the property if the ALTCS beneficiary has been permanently institutionalized. *See ARS 36-2935.* This is called a TEFRA lien, which stands for the Tax Equity and Fiscal Responsibility Act. The lien prohibits a sale or transfer of the home until the benefits paid by ALTCS for the care of the homeowner are returned.

Before any lien is filed, AHCCCS will send a Notice of Intent to File a Lien against Real Property to the AHCCCS beneficiary or the beneficiary's representative. After the filing of the lien, no further action is taken by AHCCCS until either (1) the applicant returns home with the intention of remaining home, (2) the property is sold or ownership is transferred; or (3) the applicant dies.

The Arizona Medicaid Assistance Estate Recovery Program regularly updates a brochure on this topic. As of publication, you can view this brochure at **www.azahcccs.gov/community/Downloads/Publications/DE-810_english.pdf**.

If the applicant is married, the State will not attempt to collect on the lien until after the death of the surviving spouse, and then only if the applicant is not survived by a child under 21, or disabled. Otherwise, the State may collect on the lien to the extent of the applicant's interest in the property. Whoever inherits the home must pay off the lien amount or the State could force a sale to get it.

Even if a TEFRA lien was not placed on the property prior to the applicant's death, the State could do so after death if the applicant received ALTCS benefits in a nursing home for at least 90 days after attaining age 55. *See Regulation R9-28-918.* Although uncommon, if the estate requires a probate action, the personal representative must notify the State within 3 months after the applicant's death that it has a right to file a claim against the estate by calling the applicant's caseworker. *See ARS 36-2935(B).* The only exceptions are if the applicant had not attained age 55 or the State had already filed its claim with the estate.

If the home is transferred without any probate action – such as by a beneficiary deed – the State is not likely to pursue the claim although there is uncertainty whether the State is even allowed to pursue it. The Estate Recovery Program brochure states, "AHCCCS' estate claim is filed only against the property owned by the ALTCS member at the time of his/her death that is subject to small estate affidavit or probate. This means that AHCCCS' claim is filed only against the "estate" of the individual." This implies a home could be transferred by beneficiary deed without an AHCCCS claim.

Further, in some cases AHCCCS will waive its claim or reduce its amount. A person responsible for administering the estate may apply for a waiver or reduction of the estate claim by submitting a written request to Health Management Systems, Inc. within 30 days from the date shown on the Notification of the claim. AHCCCS will make a decision within 60 days.

The only other asset at stake under the Estate Recovery Program is an annuity that is subject to probate. This would only occur when no beneficiary is designated, or when all of the named beneficiaries predecease the annuitant.

The rules are more complex than stated here. More detailed information about the TEFRA liens and its exemptions are available in the Estate Recovery Program brochure. For additional information, contact an elder law attorney to interpret the current regulations to know whether the State has the right to collect the lien against property of an ALTCS applicant.

How do I know if the State intends to file a claim against the deceased person's home?

The State would proceed by filing a Demand for Notice with the local probate court. *See ARS 14-3204.* This means that a copy of any probate filings will have to be sent by the personal representative to AHCCCS or its collection agent.

AHCCCS will send the personal representative or an authorized representative (1) a Notice of Intent to File a Claim against the Estate, (2) an Estate Questionnaire, and (3) a copy of the Demand for Notice as filed. The questionnaire will help the State identify if there are any exemptions. If no exemptions apply, the State will proceed to file a claim against the estate. The claim will be enforced if there is a probate action to transfer an asset.

Chapter 6

Transfer Assets

Once you have determined the primary approach for administering the estate, dealt with all notice and creditor issues, and identified the beneficiaries, it is time to proceed with the actual distribution process. The required steps will vary depending on the type of asset and its titling. The process of transferring assets is aided by experience. However, with reasonable effort, anyone can learn the steps and complete them.

REAL ESTATE

How do I transfer real estate subject to probate?

When a property in Arizona is "subject to" probate, it does not automatically mean that a petition must be filed with the probate court to open an informal probate. Arizona law provides a "small estate" alternative for real estate when the value of the deceased person's total interest in Arizona real estate is below a certain amount.

If the entire value of the deceased person's interest in real property is worth less than $100,000, then each property interest otherwise subject to probate may be transferred using an Affidavit of Succession to Real Property. *See ARS 14-3971(E)*.

When determining the value of a deceased person's interest in real property, the fair market value is not used to calculate the amount of equity. Rather, under Arizona law, the amount of equity is calculated by using the current year's assessed value for property tax purposes less any outstanding debt. *See ARS 14-3971(E).* Specifically, the statute refers to "the full cash value of the property as shown on the assessment rolls for the year in which the decedent died." This amount is sometimes substantially different than the fair market value. For example, the fair market value may be $250,000, but the assessed value for property tax purposes only $195,000.

The main drawback of using an Affidavit of Succession to Real Property is the affiant must wait six months after the owner's death before filing it. Often the better approach – although more expensive – is to petition for informal probate anyway because it can be opened (and closed) before the six month waiting period would have ended. Most beneficiaries prefer to sell the property to a third party rather than live in it or use it as an investment. Using an informal probate will permit a faster closing than using the small estate affidavit.

What are the requirements for using the small estate affidavit for real property?

The person signing the Affidavit of Succession to Real Property must verify all of the following statements are true:

1. The value of all of the deceased owner's interest in all real property owned in Arizona is no greater than $100,000.
2. The owner's death occurred at least six months before the filing of the affidavit.
3. No one has petitioned to become a personal representative for the estate, or if one was appointed, the estate has been closed for at least one year.
4. There are no estate taxes due from the estate.
5. The affiant is entitled to receive the property.
6. Funeral expenses, expenses of last illness, and all unsecured debts of the owner have been paid.

For very small estates – where the home is basically the only asset – this last item can be a problem. Unsecured debts include credit card debts, which normally might be written off by the credit card company. It is important to remember that the property is not technically avoiding probate. The affidavit is a probate action, so it passes subject to the claims of creditors.

The person who signs the affidavit will be the person who inherits the property, not necessarily the personal representative. If more than one person is entitled to the property, then both must sign the affidavit unless one signs a consent waiver.

Filing the affidavit is a two step process. First, the affidavit is filed in the probate court in the county where the property is located, along with a certified copy of the death certificate, and the original will if there is one. Second, a certified copy of the affidavit must be recorded in the same county.

The affidavit procedure is more complicated than it initially appears. Although you may have little trouble locating the appropriate affidavit, the filing requirements are so precise that it will probably save you time and frustration if you retain an estate attorney to assist you.

What if the property has an outstanding mortgage?

The typical mortgage will state that any transfer of the property will trigger a due-on-sale clause. In other words, the mortgage becomes due and payable immediately upon sale or transfer. Thus, the beneficiary of the property should contact the mortgage lender before making a transfer using the Affidavit of Succession to Real Property. The mortgage lender does not have to agree to use of the affidavit procedure. It may prefer a traditional probate action in order to refinance the mortgage.

What if the property does not qualify for use of the small estate affidavit?

In order to transfer a property to a beneficiary as part of a probate, the personal representative will sign and record a deed of distribution. The deed will identify the estate as "grantor" and the beneficiary as "grantee." If there are multiple beneficiaries, it is good practice to clarify how the grantees will own the property. For example, the grantees may inherit the property as "tenants-in-common." This means they each own an equal, undivided interest in the property. After recording of the deed of distribution, the beneficiary is free to sell or use the property.

What if the property has a beneficiary deed?

A beneficiary deed eliminates the need for any probate action, provided it was properly recorded prior to the owner's death. *See ARS 33-405.*

Although some estate attorneys prefer to record a brief affidavit to formalize the process, the only requirement is that a death certificate be recorded in the county where the property is located. This will serve as evidence that the beneficiary deed is in effect and the property ownership has changed.

What if the property is held as joint tenants with right of survivorship?

For property held as "joint tenants with right of survivorship", assuming one of the joint owners is still living, an affidavit should be recorded to show the change in ownership. The affidavit – referred to as an Affidavit Evidencing Termination of Joint Tenancy – removes the deceased owner's name from the deed. The affidavit is not technically required. However, the failure to record either the affidavit or at least a death certificate leaves a "cloud" on the title. Eventually when the property is sold, refinanced, or transferred at the death of the surviving owner, someone will need to address the fact that the first owner died previously. The best practice is to record the affidavit when documentation is readily available. Another reason to record the affidavit is failure to do so might leave the door open to a new claim against the deceased owner's estate after death.

If the property has two or more surviving joint owners, the joint tenancy with right of survivorship relationship continues. However, an affidavit should still be recorded with a certified copy of the death certificate.

What if the property is held as community property with right of survivorship?

The process is similar for property held as community property with right of survivorship. Upon the death of husband or wife, the surviving spouse should record an affidavit terminating the right of survivorship. The property is no longer community property and would be subject to probate upon the death of the surviving spouse, unless the spouse transfers the property to a trust or records a beneficiary deed prior to death.

How do I transfer property owned by an Arizona resident but located outside Arizona?

Each state has its own requirements and procedures. You may have to consult with an estate attorney in the state where the property is located.

Most states do not require any filings in the event a joint owner of property dies, assuming there is a right of survivorship. For example, if the deceased owner was married, and they held title to a vacation property in Michigan, the surviving spouse likely need not record anything. It is good practice to record a certified copy of the death certificate in the county where the property is located, but even that may not be necessary as long as the surviving spouse can present a death certificate when the property is later sold, refinanced or transferred. In other states, an affidavit may be required so that the change of ownership is very clear. You might want to call the county recorder where the property is located to find out what the standard practice is.

If the property was owned solely by the deceased person, or if the deceased's interest was not subject to a right of survivorship, then a probate action is likely required. Most, if not all, states have some sort of procedure to simplify the process if the value of the deceased owner's interest does not exceed a defined value. Some Internet research or a call to an estate attorney in that state should provide the needed information.

If a probate is opened in Arizona, then the personal representative can use the Letters of Personal Representative to open an ancillary (or secondary) probate in the other state and transfer the property. On the other hand, if no probate is required in Arizona, the personal representative might need to petition for appointment as personal representative in the other state if the state's laws dictate such action. For example, consider the possibility that the deceased owner had previously inherited a one-third undivided interest in a farm back in Ohio. The deceased owner's father left the property to his three children as part of his estate plan. Without a right of survivorship, the deceased owner's interest must be valued and compared to the amount of any small estate exemption to determine whether a probate action in Ohio is required.

How do I transfer vacation timeshares?

Most vacation timeshare interests are treated as real estate. Thus, you will need to learn the law in the state where the timeshare interest is deeded and proceed as if it was a regular piece of property. The best way to start is to call the resort or timeshare company directly to get advice on what to do.

They may know the standard procedure and even refer you to someone who can help with the process.

The vast majority of vacation timeshare interests have a fair market value well below the initial purchase price. This increases the likelihood that a small estate affidavit will be sufficient to transfer the interest. Unless you are certain the vacation timeshare interest has substantial fair market value, it likely will not trigger a probate action by itself. However, if there are other assets subject to probate, then the vacation timeshare interest should be included on the list of probate assets.

A growing percentage of vacation timeshare interests are not deeded, but rather subject to a written "points" contract that may clarify who inherits the remaining interest.

Transfers of vacation timeshare interests usually incur a nominal transfer fee – perhaps $100 to $300 – payable to the management company. There may also be substantial costs to prepare and record a small estate affidavit or deed of distribution.

Vacation timeshare interests are often titled in the name of living trusts. A successor trustee may proceed to transfer the timeshare interest to a beneficiary without any probate action, although there will likely be a nominal transfer fee. Also, many vacation timeshare interests deeded in Arizona are held subject to a beneficiary deed.

If the person responsible for administering the estate learns that none of the beneficiaries actually wants to take ownership of the vacation timeshare interest, then a sale or gift of the interest is possible. This usually occurs when the beneficiaries are informed how expensive the annual maintenance fees are.

The simplest option is to assign the ownership interest back to the resort or timeshare company. Another option is to list the timeshare for sale with a company specializing in re-sales. But beware, some timeshare re-sale companies are notorious for promising more than they can deliver. A third option is to contact a company in the business of purchasing timeshare interests. Just be prepared to pay a hefty transfer fee for the privilege of selling the interest. But at least the beneficiaries need not continue paying the annual maintenance fees for something they do not plan to use.

Other options include offering the timeshare for sale – or gift – in a local newspaper or on popular websites like e-Bay or Craigslist. Also, a small number of charities actively pursue timeshares in order to sell them and keep the profit.

What if the deceased person was a resident of another state, but had property in Arizona?

If the owner of real property in Arizona died as a resident of another state, the property is subject to the same laws applicable to property owned by Arizona residents.

The best case in this scenario is for the property to be held in the name of a living trust. In fact, the value of a living trust is most evident when a person owns real property in more than one state. The successor trustee need only record an affidavit to disclose the original trustee's death and then proceed to record a deed of distribution in the county where the property is located. The deed of distribution transfers the property to the beneficiary. If the property is held subject to a mortgage, then the transfer process can be handled entirely by a title company when the loan is refinanced in the name of the beneficiary.

If the property is not held in a living trust, but the value of the deceased owner's interest in the property is less than $100,000, then an Affidavit of Succession to Real Property may be used to transfer ownership. However, if the value of the deceased owner's interest is more than $100,000, or if the use of an affidavit procedure is not permitted by the mortgage lender, then a probate action is required.

The type of probate action will also depend on whether a personal representative was appointed in another state. If a probate action is not required in the state where the owner resided, then the process begins much like it would for an Arizona resident. However, if a personal representative was already appointed in another state, then there is a simpler probate action the personal representative can use to transfer the Arizona property.

The personal representative can petition for "Proof of Authority" from the probate court in the county where the Arizona property is located. *See ARS 14-4204.* The Proof of Authority still requires filing with the appropriate Arizona probate court, but the filing piggy-backs on the probate case already open in the other state.

If the petition for Proof of Authority is approved, the Arizona probate court will add yet another title to the person responsible for administering the estate: "domiciliary foreign personal representative." Now the personal representative appointed in another state is permitted to exercise any of the powers of a personal representative who was initially appointed in Arizona. *See ARS 14-4205.*

When filing the petition for Proof of Authority, the Arizona probate court will require a copy of Letters of Personal Representative from the other state, certified within the past 60 days, a copy of the bond, or if waived in a will, then a certified copy of the will. The filing fee varies by county, but is approximately $200 to $250. When approved, the probate court will return a certified copy of the Proof of Authority. The personal representative then records the certified Proof of Authority in the county where the property is located. The last step is to record a Deed of Distribution, which publicly identifies the new owner of the property.

BANK AND CREDIT UNION ACCOUNTS, CDs, SAVINGS, ETC.

How do I collect the deceased person's unpaid wages?

Although rare, it is possible that the deceased person was employed at the time of death and the employer stops payment of the final paycheck until the surviving spouse opens a probate. Under Arizona law, a surviving spouse may instead present an Affidavit for Collection of Wages to the employer immediately after the deceased spouse's death and request that the final paycheck is paid directly to the surviving spouse. *See ARS 14-3971(A).* The final paycheck may include unused vacation pay and sick time pay, although the affidavit is only useful when the total amount paid is less than $5,000.

If the amount is more than $5,000, or if there is no surviving spouse, then the person responsible for administering the estate will need to present a copy of the Letters of Personal Representative obtained by probate action, or an Affidavit for Collection of Personal Property, if agreed upon.

What are the requirements for using the small estate affidavit for money accounts?

The counterpart to the Affidavit for Succession to Real Property is the Affidavit for Collection of Personal Property." It is a highly useful tool for closing out small accounts without much hassle. *See ARS 14-3971(C).* Most financial institutions will be eager to accept it.

In fact, the biggest hassle you might run into is responding to a customer service agent at a financial institution who is not familiar with use of small estate affidavits. The agent might follow protocol and request Letters of Personal Representative before a more experienced agent or supervisor agrees later to accept the affidavit.

Unlike the six month waiting period applicable to the Affidavit for Succession to Real Property, the waiting period to use the Affidavit for Collection of Personal Property is only 30 days after date of death.

The person signing the affidavit must verify all of the following statements are true:

1. The value of all of the deceased person's personal property owned in Arizona is no greater than $75,000.
2. The owner's death occurred at least 30 days before the submission of the affidavit.
3. No one has petitioned to become a personal representative for the estate, or if one was appointed, the estate has been closed for at least one year.
4. The affiant is entitled to receive the property.

Note that a deceased person's personal property includes the value of all financial accounts – but only those subject to probate – regardless of where the financial institution is located.

The affidavit is not filed anywhere, but instead is presented to the financial institution. By law, a financial institution is released from liability when it transfers an account to the person or persons identified in the affidavit.

This small estate affidavit is an excellent tool to bypass the probate process in Arizona. However, in some cases, a person responsible for administering an estate might choose not to use it. A probate may be preferred when there are creditors to deal with and the personal representative needs to gather funds in order to pay debts, expenses of the estate, or to satisfy specific bequests. If the personal representative transfers all of the deceased person's accounts directly to a beneficiary or beneficiaries, then the funds are unavailable to the personal representative.

How do I transfer an account with a pay-on-death or transfer-on-death designation?

It is not difficult to transfer accounts with pay-on-death and transfer-on-death designations. The designated beneficiary should contact the financial institution and ask for its procedure to close or transfer the account.

It is not necessary for the person responsible for administering the estate to handle this task. The beneficiary could do it alone, provided the beneficiary has a certified copy of the death certificate to present to the financial institution.

How do I transfer a motor vehicle?

The title of a motor vehicle registered in Arizona can be transferred at any office of the Motor Vehicle Division. If the person responsible for administering the estate is out-of-state, then it may be worth contacting an authorized MVD service provider to handle the matter in Arizona. For example, some AAA offices in Arizona offer this service.

If the motor vehicle qualifies for use of an Affidavit for Collection of Personal Property, then a person qualified to receive the motor vehicle may submit the affidavit. The MVD version of the form is available on the MVD website. *See Form #32-6901, "Non-Probate Affidavit"* at **www.azdot.gov/mvd/.**

If a probate action is required, the personal representative takes a certified copy of the Letters of Personal Representative to a local MVD office and applies for a new title in either the name of the estate or directly in the name of a beneficiary.

If a third party wants to buy the motor vehicle, the affiant or personal representative, as the case may be, could meet the buyer at the MVD office and handle both transactions simultaneously.

If the owner of the motor vehicle was still making payments on it, the process is more complicated. The person responsible for administering the estate will have to contact the lender, obtain a copy of the loan document, and determine the available options. The MVD will not transfer title until a lien release is presented, and the lender will not issue it until the loan is paid off or assigned to the new owner. The MVD provides a lien release form on its website. *See MVD Form #48-9901.*

Although rarely used, it is possible that the deceased owner designated a beneficiary of the motor vehicle. *See ARS 28-2055(B).* If a title is presented with a beneficiary designation form stapled to it, the MVD will re-issue title in the name of the beneficiary upon presentation of a death certificate.

When the motor vehicle is transferred, the license plate should be returned to a MVD office, not left on the vehicle.

What do I do with a leased car?

A leased motor vehicle is a liability to the estate. The deceased person's estate still has an obligation to pay the balance of the contract whether anyone drives the motor vehicle or not. There are a few options. The person responsible for administering the estate could ask if the leasing company will assign the balance of the lease to someone else, or could negotiate a lump sum payment to end the lease. The amount of the lump sum is usually determined according to a formula in the fine print of the lease agreement. The latter option could be rather expensive, and feel unfair, but it generally is the best option. As for assigning the lease, there is a small but growing market for lease assignments. For example, visit **www.swapalease.com**.

If the deceased owner has no assets subject to creditor claims, another option is to just bring the car back to the leasing company and refuse to pay the remaining obligation. Although the leasing company could sue the estate, there would be nothing for them to get. Of course there is an obvious exception to this statement. If the lease is treated as a community debt with a surviving spouse, the leasing company could make a claim against the spouse's share of the community property and the spouse's separate property if he or she signed the lease. Thus, in Arizona, the option to just bring the car back to the leasing company and refuse further payment is reserved for situations where the deceased person was unmarried and left no assets subject to the claims of creditors.

If a beneficiary chooses to keep the car and intends to drive it regularly, then the beneficiary should be added as a named insured on the insurance policy.

How do I transfer government savings bonds?

The Treasury Direct website provides forms to liquidate or transfer U.S. savings bonds and other government issued investments after the death of an owner. **www.treasurydirect.gov** This website also describes the various types of bonds, notes, and securities issued by the federal government, which can be helpful when sorting through a deceased person's assets.

Savings bonds are labeled by series. For example, electronic issue bonds are referred to as Series E, EE or I. Paper issue bonds or notes are referred to as Series A, B, C, D, E, EE, F, G, H, HH, I, J, or K. The Treasury Direct website includes forms to transfer all of these investments, plus government-issued marketable securities, bonds, and notes. Series E, EE, and I bonds may also be transferred at most banks in person.

Savings bonds that have not reached the final maturity date may be reissued under new ownership. However, all other bonds must be redeemed.

For bonds and securities issued in the name of the deceased owner, the personal representative should submit Form PD-F-1455-E in order to make payment to the estate, living trust, or directly to the beneficiaries. This same form is used when distributing bonds and securities held in the name of the deceased person's living trust.

If the bonds and securities qualify for use of an Affidavit for Collection of Personal Property, the affiant should submit Form PD-F-5394 in order to make payment directly to the beneficiary.

When there is a surviving joint owner, the deceased person's name is removed from the title using Form PD-F-5336-E.

All forms require a Medallion Guarantee of the signature. This is different from a notary public's signature. Most bank branches will have someone – usually the branch manager – who is capable of issuing a Medallion Guarantee.

For specific instructions about how to administer U.S. bonds and other government-issued investments, read Form PD-P-0064 if a traditional probate is required or Form PD-P0065 if not.

LIFE INSURANCE

What do I do with life insurance policies?

Life insurance is one of the most common assets held by a deceased person. Even the elderly grandparent with no dependents is likely to own one or more small, paid-up life insurance policies. Other people acquire small life insurance policies from military service or through a credit union membership.

The person responsible for administering the estate should collect any documentation that refers to life insurance of the deceased person. There is a tendency to find life insurance policies in strange places at unexpected times. Of course, it is better to find a policy sooner rather than later, so look carefully. The deceased person's bank and credit union statements often show evidence of premium payments, but many policies are already paid up; i.e., premium payments are no longer required. Another good practice is to ask the deceased person's property insurance agent, financial advisor, and estate attorney whether they are aware of any other life insurance policies. If still employed, the deceased person's employer may also be aware of a life insurance policy that does not show up on bank statements.

The best place to start the claim process is to contact the insurance agent who sold each policy, but if the agent cannot be reached, then contact each insurance company. Your top priority should be verifying the beneficiary designation for each policy. In order to file a claim, a form will need to be completed along with delivery of a certified copy of the death certificate. The form and instructions are usually available on the company website.

When a claim is paid, the check will be made payable to the beneficiary or beneficiaries. Thus, the life insurance company will need to know each beneficiary's address, and probably the date of birth and social security number too. This process is pretty straight-forward in most cases, but will not be when a minor child or incapacitated adult is a beneficiary.

In many cases a trust is named as the beneficiary. If the owner's living trust is the beneficiary, then the claimant is the successor trustee. The check should be deposited into an account titled in the name of the trust before it is distributed pursuant to the terms of the trust document. In other cases, a trust created by will after the death of the insured will be named as beneficiary. The person designated as trustee in the will should open an account in the name of the beneficiary's new trust before filing the claim with the life insurance company.

Life insurance proceeds are not taxable to the beneficiary, at least for income tax purposes. The exemption is unlimited so even a $2 million death benefit could be inherited free of income tax. On the other hand, life insurance proceeds are subject to estate tax. Avoiding the estate tax is a common motive for using an advanced estate planning technique called the irrevocable life insurance trust. With this technique a special trust is established during the deceased person's lifetime, which becomes the owner and beneficiary of a life insurance policy. When the person dies, the policy proceeds are paid to the trustee who can use the funds to purchase assets from the deceased person's estate. The objective is to provide liquidity to the estate so it can afford to pay the estate taxes.

ANNUITIES

How do I know if annuity payments stop after the owner's death?

Annuities are very popular investments by the elderly, so they are common assets for survivors to deal with after the death of a loved one. A traditional annuity provides a regular income stream to the beneficiary for a term of years or for lifetime. Other "deferred" annuities permit accumulation of investment gains until a later date when payments to the beneficiary begin. The payment amount is calculated using the age and life expectancy of a person, who is referred to as the annuitant. The owner can be almost anyone, including a living trust, but is usually the annuitant. From an investment perspective, annuities can be very complicated. Although some annuities are very simple and easy to understand, the myriad of options and investment choices can make the topic very complex to even the most financially astute.

Some annuities are owned inside Individual Retirement Arrangements ("IRAs"). The IRA "wrapper" makes the situation even more complex because annuity payments might be collected inside the IRA before coming out as IRA distributions to the owner.

The good news is that annuities are not as complicated after the owner's death as they are during lifetime. Every annuity has a beneficiary designation with a death beneficiary, which should be fairly simple to interpret. In most cases the death beneficiary is identified on the initial application, although the owner may change the beneficiary designation prior to death. The beneficiary of record must be confirmed by the annuity company.

In order to determine what the beneficiary receives, one must know whether the annuity was in the accumulation phase or payout phase at the annuitant's death. The accumulation phase is the period before the beneficiary begins to receive regular payments from the contract. The payout phase is the period during which the beneficiary receives regular payments, usually monthly. This should be somewhat obvious by looking at a recent statement from the annuity administrator. If the statement shows regular distributions out to an account owned by the deceased person, then you know the annuity is in payout phase. If the answer is not clear, then contact the annuity administrator to find out.

The distinction between accumulation and payout phase is very important. For the annuity in accumulation phase, the beneficiary is entitled to the current balance of the account (or premiums paid, if more) plus any additional death benefit outlined in the contract. For example, an annuity in accumulation phase may have $73,000 in investments and a $100,000 death benefit. In this case, the death beneficiary would receive $173,000. However, many annuities do not offer an additional death benefit if the annuity was still in accumulation phase.

For the annuity in payout phase, as it often is for elderly persons, there will not be a death benefit but rather a payout option identified in the contract itself. The basic options available to the annuity owner at the start of the payout phase are:

Life Only
- Payments end when annuitant dies.

Life with Period Certain
- Payments might continue to beneficiary after annuitant's death if guaranteed number of payments has not been reached, usually 10 or 20 years.

Joint and Survivor
- Payments continue for the surviving person designated in the contract; the payments end when that person dies.

If the deceased person was the surviving beneficiary from a contract held with a predeceased person, then the payments would end.

What are the pay-out options for annuity death benefits?

For an annuity not in payout phase, a non-spouse beneficiary usually has three options for how to receive the annuity payout.

- Lump sum distribution (aka "Blow-out").

- Annuitize the distribution over the beneficiary's life expectancy or a period of years (aka "Stretch-out").

- Entire amount must be distributed by the 5th anniversary date of the owner's date of death (aka "Five Year Rule").

The Stretch-out option is only available to individual beneficiaries, not trusts (contrary to similar IRA regulations). However, some companies permit the annuity owner to establish a "control payout" option, which restricts the beneficiary's access to funds while still distributing enough to satisfy requirements.

A spouse beneficiary has the same three options plus an additional option to continue the contract. The surviving spouse would become the new owner and annuitant.

RETIREMENT ACCOUNTS

What happens to an IRA after its owner's death?

At first glance the steps to transfer an Individual Retirement Arrangement ("IRA") may seem pretty straight-forward. The deceased person owned an investment account. The beneficiary designation says who is supposed to receive it. It all seems similar to life insurance, right? Well, yes, the beneficiary designation is the governing document and it may be simple to interpret. But there is a major difference between transfer of life insurance after the insured's death and an IRA after the owner's death: income taxes.

Are IRA distributions taxable to the beneficiary?

Yes, with the exception of Roth IRA and Roth 401k accounts, the beneficiary inherits the account and the liability for income tax as the funds are received.

Can the IRA be transferred to the beneficiary or must the IRA be closed and funds distributed?

The U.S. public policy is to promote retirement savings, and specifically the use of IRAs, by letting them operate in a tax-deferred environment. But Congress also established rules governing whether and for how long the beneficiaries may retain the IRA assets in a tax-deferred environment after the owner's death. These rules are so complicated that entire treatises are devoted to the topic.

IRAs were never intended to serve as wealth transfer vehicles. They were created by Congress to encourage retirement savings, and lessen the burden on the social security system. Thus, the simplest distribution plan – and the one the government wants you to use – is to withdraw all of your retirement savings during your retirement years and then die when your account reaches zero. However, as tax-deferred retirement accounts have become more popular during the last 25 years, it is more likely that an account owner will have money left in the retirement account when the account owner dies. From an estate planning perspective, the IRA beneficiary designation becomes an important component of an estate plan because it describes the plan of distribution for remaining funds after the owner's death.

Before proceeding further, a summary of the *lifetime* distribution rules is in order. During your working years, Congress wants you to invest a portion of your earnings into retirement savings. Congress has established a tax policy that encourages savings by giving various tax breaks to those who are able to save. The most valuable tax break is that money invested through an

IRA (or 401k, 403b, etc.) may grow income tax-deferred. Investment profits are reinvested without having to pay income tax on that profit each year. This tax-free compounding can permit extraordinary increases in value over a long period of time. But there is a catch.

Congress does not provide this tax break for free. Uncle Sam wants his share eventually. Basically, there are two choices. You can pay the income tax up front; i.e., when you deposit the money into the account (e.g., Roth IRA). Or you will have to pay income tax on the amounts you withdraw later (e.g., traditional IRA, 401k). If you take the second choice, you cannot wait forever. In fact, you must begin to take withdrawals during the year that you attain 70 1/2 years of age – even if you don't want or need to. This is called the required minimum distribution or RMD for short. Each subsequent year the tax law requires you to take a taxable distribution from your account. The initial RMD is small (in percentage), but the distributions will increase in size as you get older. The good news is that RMDs are usually small enough – especially before you reach your mid 80s – that with good investment returns your account may continue to increase in value even though you are taking out RMDs each year.

The tax laws for retirement accounts are very complex. You probably don't need to know many of the details. Here is what you should remember: RMDs are good. They achieve Congress's purpose and prevent your retirement money from eroding too quickly. RMDs are so good that you beneficiaries may want to use them too. Unfortunately, it's not that easy. Remember that Congress did not intend for tax-deferred retirement accounts to last forever. They were intended to supplement any Social Security income. In other words, if you end up being one of those people who still has a large amount of money in your IRA after death, then Congress will want your beneficiaries to withdraw the money you did not need.

For most people, when completing the beneficiary designation for a retirement account, they focus on *who* is entitled to receive the account after they die. But the real question is *how* and *when* the beneficiaries must take out this money.

What if a surviving spouse is named as beneficiary?

From a tax perspective, the best result occurs when there is a surviving spouse. A surviving spouse can "roll over" the IRA into the spouse's IRA.

This permits the spouse to wait until age 70 1/2 before starting to take RMDs. Also, a surviving spouse calculates RMDs using a different, more favorable, IRS tax table. The RMDs will be smaller than they would be for a similar age non-spouse beneficiary. A final benefit is that the spouse's life expectancy is recalculated each year so that RMDs increase at a slower pace than they would for a non-spouse beneficiary.

Can a non-spouse transfer the IRA without paying taxes right away?

No. The option to roll over an IRA is only available to a surviving spouse. A non-spouse beneficiary will usually have to begin taking minimum required distributions from the account by the end of the calendar year following the owner's death.

The required minimum distribution (RMD) rules are based on a life expectancy calculation for the beneficiary. Before the owner's death, the RMD is calculated using the owner's age and an IRS tax table that estimates the owner's life expectancy. The older the beneficiary is, the larger the RMD. After the owner's death, the RMD is calculated using the age of a beneficiary. In general, the beneficiary must be an individual, although in some cases the IRS will permit the beneficiaries of a trust to qualify for this purpose.

For example, assume Dad dies and leaves a $100,000 IRA to his 55 year old son. The IRS tax tables calculate the first year RMD using a 29.6 year life expectancy for the son. Thus, the RMD is $3,378 ($100,000 / 29.6). In other words, if the IRA investments achieve a return higher than 3.38%, then the IRA value will actually increase during the year. In year two, the son's RMD will be calculated by dividing the IRA value by 28.6 (29.6 less one each year).

What are the payout options for a non-spouse beneficiary?

When a non-spouse individual is named as beneficiary, the individual has two basic choices for how to receive the IRA assets:

- Lump sum payment
- RMDs based on life expectancy ("Stretch IRA")

A third option, called the Five Year Rule, is available when the IRA owner died before reaching age 70 1/2. Under this rule, annual distributions are not required. The only requirement is that the entire IRA must be distributed by December 31 of the year that contains the fifth anniversary of the IRA owner's death.

The lump sum payout option means that the beneficiary will treat that amount as taxable income and pay income taxes on the entire amount immediately. The after-tax balance will be owned outright by the beneficiary. Future investment income is also taxable each year.

The Stretch IRA option means that the beneficiary will receive the RMD each year until the beneficiary dies or the IRA is depleted. The younger the beneficiary is, the smaller the RMD will be. Even if the Stretch IRA option is chosen, the beneficiary may choose to take out more than the RMD at any time. There is nothing to prevent the beneficiary from depleting the account.

Some retirement plans will not provide all the options available by law. Many employer sponsored plans (401k, 403b, etc.) will mandate the lump sum payment, even though they are permitted to offer the Five Year Rule or life expectancy payout option. And the author is aware of at least one major IRA provider that does not offer the Stretch IRA option. However, a recent law change now requires employer sponsored plans to permit transfer to an inherited IRA in order to obtain the Stretch IRA benefits.

What responsibilities do I have to the other beneficiaries of an IRA?

As the estate administrator you should counsel the beneficiaries of any retirement accounts to examine their options carefully. If you are a beneficiary, then you should get your own counsel regarding your options. There are major tax ramifications regarding *how* a beneficiary takes money out of a retirement account. Taking the money as a lump sum may be just fine, but do not assume it is the only way.

When an individual is named as beneficiary, the beneficiary has all of the control. Even if you know the Stretch IRA option is best, there is no way to compel a named beneficiary to choose this option. In addition, the beneficiary can spend inherited IRA money on whatever he or she chooses, even if the beneficiary's behavior conflicts with the customized distribution plan described in the deceased owner's will or living trust.

What if the IRA is payable to a trust?

Some IRAs name a trust as beneficiary. There is nothing wrong with this from a legal perspective. In fact, it may make perfect sense if the owner wants to protect the inheritance of a minor, incapacitated, or otherwise irresponsible beneficiary.

However, a trust, in general, does not qualify for the Stretch IRA option because it is not an individual with a life expectancy. In order to make a trust qualify, the trust must meet specific requirements. If they are met, then the IRS permits the IRA custodian to identify the beneficiaries by "looking through" the trust. Unless sub-trusts are identified separately in the beneficiary designation itself, the IRA will make RMDs using the life expectancy of the oldest trust beneficiary. When drafted correctly, it is perfectly acceptable to name a trust as beneficiary. The document must comply with all the appropriate tax rules, but otherwise there are no restrictions on what it may provide, other than what the IRA custodian will approve.

A growing number of IRAs are made payable to so-called IRA trusts. These trusts are specifically drafted to deal with retirement plan accounts. They are intended to insure the availability of Stretch IRA provisions, maximize creditor protection for the beneficiaries, and provide ongoing professional management of the investments.

What if the IRA beneficiary is a charity?

Yes, a charitable organization may be designated as beneficiary of an IRA. In fact, it may be a great idea. A tax-exempt charity does not have to deal with any of the aforementioned income tax issues. The entire account will be available to the charity.

CORPORATE INTERESTS

How do I transfer stock of a closely-held Arizona corporation?

If the deceased person was an officer or statutory agent of an Arizona corporation, you will need to update the records of the corporation with the Arizona Corporation Commission at **www.cc.state.az.us**. This information can be updated on the next annual report, but it is good practice to appoint a new statutory agent as soon as possible. The statutory agent is the person who receives correspondence on behalf of the corporation. The appropriate forms are available on the ACC website.

If you have identified the beneficiary of the corporate stock, you may proceed to transfer the stock of a closely-held Arizona corporation by assigning the stock certificate to its new owner. If you cannot locate a minute book with stock certificates, look for a copy of the prior tax return for the corporation. The accountant should know who the shareholders are and be able to help create stock certificates going forward. In other cases the stock will be redeemed by the corporation or purchased by the other shareholder pursuant to a buy-sell agreement. An amendment to the articles of incorporation may or may not be necessary. You may consult with an estate or business attorney to be sure.

How do I transfer membership interests of a closely-held Arizona limited liability company?

If the deceased person was a member, manager, or statutory agent of an Arizona limited liability company (LLC), you will need to update the records of the corporation with the Arizona Corporation Commission at **www.cc.state.az.us**. If the LLC is member-managed, or if manager-managed and the deceased person owned more than 20% of the membership interests, then you will need to amend the articles of organization to disclose the new membership. The appropriate forms are available on the ACC website.

TRANSFERS TO MINOR CHILDREN AND INCAPACITATED ADULTS

Property should not be distributed outright to a minor child. If a minor child is supposed to receive property, the person responsible for administering the estate has up to three options. Sometimes the governing document, applicable law, and value of the property dictate which choices are available.

What is the best option for distributing money to a minor child?

The best option by far is to leave the property in trust for benefit of the child. A trust provides maximum flexibility and privacy. To illustrate, note how the other two available options – custodianship and conservatorship accounts – require outright distribution of the asset at age 18 or 21. A trust can be drafted to retain assets in trust until any age or for the beneficiary's lifetime. A trust can also be established for multiple beneficiaries, a feature not available with custodianship or conservatorship accounts. A trust for a minor child is managed by an adult or trust company (the "trustee"), who does not have to file any reports with the probate court.

Unfortunately, the trust option is only available if the governing document permits it. The governing document may be a will, living trust, or beneficiary designation. In some cases the governing document might explicitly choose the trust option. For example, the deceased person's will document might say, "My personal representative shall retain the share for Child in trust until Child attains age 30." The absence of such language does not necessarily prevent the use of a trust. A separate administrative provision could give the personal representative discretion to put the funds in trust instead of giving them outright to Child. For example, *see ARS 14-10819.* Also, in many wills and living trusts prepared by estate attorneys, the personal representative or trustee may distribute small amounts directly to a parent or guardian of Child. This could be the simplest option of all.

If no trust option, then how do I transfer money to a minor child?

The answer depends first on the source of the distribution. Is the distribution described in a will, living trust, beneficiary designation, or directed by Arizona intestacy laws? You will need to examine the appropriate document or law to determine whether it provides specific instructions for how to distribute funds to a minor child. For example, a will might say, "I give $25,000 to Adult, as custodian for Child under the Arizona Uniform Transfers to Minors Act." *See ARS 14-7651 et. al.* This is the second option for leaving property to a minor child. Gifts made subject to the Arizona UTMA permit an adult to manage the funds for benefit of a child. The child is entitled to outright ownership of the funds upon attaining age 21 if the custodianship was authorized by a will or trust, or age 18 if by another governing document or the discretion of a personal representative or trustee. Besides a will and trust, a distribution subject to the Arizona UTMA could be made by deed, beneficiary designation, or by exercising a power of appointment.

When a custodianship is established, the person responsible for administering the estate should examine the governing document in case the deceased person nominated an adult to serve as custodian. Under *ARS 14-7655(B)*, the personal representative or trustee must transfer the money to that person as custodian. If, however, the governing document fails to nominate an adult or if the nominated person is unable or unwilling to serve as custodian, then the personal representative or trustee may choose an adult or trust company to do so. An adult custodian need not be a member of the minor's family.

If the minor child resides outside Arizona, the transfer can still be made to an Arizona account subject to UTMA, provided the property is located in Arizona at the time of the transfer. *See ARS 14-7652(A)*. If the property is located outside Arizona, the laws of the state where the minor child resides are applicable. This should not be much of an issue because the custodianship rules are fairly uniform from state to state.

What if the trust option is not available and there is no governing document that mentions custodianship?

If the governing document fails to mention the Arizona Uniform Transfers to Minors Act, or if the deceased person did not leave a valid will and the Arizona intestacy laws apply, then a personal representative or trustee may still be able to use the UTMA option. The personal representative or trustee could distribute the money, without court involvement, to an adult custodian under the Arizona UTMA, provided (1) the personal representative or trustee considers the transfer to be in the best interest of the child, (2) the transfer is not prohibited by or inconsistent with the terms of the governing document, and (3) the dollar amount is less than $10,000. *See ARS 14-7656.*

What if the money is going to be paid out by an insurance company or financial institution?

A similar statute applies when a company must pay funds to a minor child pursuant to a life insurance policy or where a minor child is the named beneficiary of a financial account. Provided the distribution amount is less than $10,000, the company may transfer the funds to an adult nominated as custodian for the child in the applicable beneficiary designation, or the deceased person's will or living trust. If no custodian has been nominated, then the company may transfer the money to any adult member of the minor child's family or to a trust company. *See ARS 14-7657*.

However, if the distribution amount exceeds $10,000, then the company cannot transfer the money without authorization from a probate court. *See ARS 14-7657(C)*. In fact, the company might still request authorization from a probate court for amounts less than $10,000.

In summary, the Arizona UTMA is a simple solution for any size distribution amount if the governing document expressly refers to UTMA. It also works well when there is no such authorization, especially if the distribution amount is less than $10,000.

What is the default option?

The default option is a conservatorship. This option provides some oversight to the management of funds for the child. It might also be useful for management of funds for an adult beneficiary when outright distribution is not in the best interests of the beneficiary.

A conservatorship begins with the appointment of an adult by the probate court to serve as conservator of the child's property. The appointment process is rather complicated and usually requires an attorney familiar with it. Establishing a conservatorship may incur substantial costs and frustrate a person unfamiliar with this area of law. For these reasons, estate attorneys rarely suggest the use of a conservatorship when a client makes an estate plan.

The first step is to determine whether a conservator has already been appointed for the child. If there is one, then the funds can be paid directly to the conservator, even if the conservator or minor resides in another state.

If a conservatorship needs to be established, then an interested person must petition a probate court in the state where the child resides to appoint an adult as conservator for the child's property. The conservator is usually a parent of the child or a financial institution. Depending on the court rules for that state, the probate court may schedule a hearing to determine whether the prospective conservator is qualified to serve. In Arizona, if the child is 14 years of age or older, the court will consider the child's preference in deciding who the court will appoint as conservator. Once appointed, the conservator has full control of the child's property, although the conservator must abide by strict fiduciary standards and reporting requirements. The costs to maintain the conservatorship are paid for out of the child's funds. When the child attains age 18, the child or the conservator must petition the court to end the conservatorship and release any remaining funds to the child.

An attorney experienced in conservatorships can assist with filing the petition with the court to appoint a conservator. Strict notice and bond requirements must be met. In Arizona, within 90 days of appointment, the conservator must file an inventory of the assets under conservatorship. Annual accountings are also required. *See ARS 14-5404, ARS 14-5405, ARS 14-5412, and ARS 14-5419.*

What if the beneficiary is an incapacitated adult?

In general, any distribution to an incapacitated adult should be transferred to a conservator. The process is similar to a conservatorship for a minor child, although in this case the probate court must make one of the following determinations before appointing a conservator:

- The person is unable to manage his or her estate and affairs effectively for reasons such as mental illness, mental deficiency, mental disorder, physical illness or disability, chronic use of drugs, chronic intoxication, confinement, detention by a foreign power or disappearance, or

- The person has property which will be wasted or dissipated unless proper management is provided, or that funds are needed for the support, care and welfare of the person or those entitled to be supported by the person and that protection is necessary or desirable to obtain or provide funds.

If the beneficiary already has a conservator, property may be distributed directly to the conservator.

There may be another option. If the governing document – a will, trust, power of appointment, or beneficiary designation – provides that distributions to incapacitated adults may be transferred to a trust, then this is likely a better choice. The document may even include detailed provisions for a special needs trust. This type of trust is intended to provide benefits to a beneficiary without causing the beneficiary to lose public benefits he or she is entitled to receive. The trust is designed in such a way that the beneficiary cannot unilaterally take property out of the trust. An independent trustee has complete discretion over distributions from the trust. For additional information about special needs trusts, contact the Special Needs Alliance. **www.specialneedsalliance.org**.

Chapter 7

Close the Estate

Once you have distributed all of the assets out of the deceased person's name, you are ready to close the estate. In the case of a probate, you must wait at least four months after the notice to creditors was first published, even if you have already distributed all of the assets. In the case of a living trust, there are no time restrictions unless they were self-imposed by a voluntary notice to creditors. If the trust no longer owns anything, then the trust terminates. In either case your final tasks usually involve the completion of accountings and tax returns.

PROBATE

How does an informal probate end?

The most common method of closing an informal probate is by filing a closing statement with the court. *See ARS 14-3933.* The closing statement cannot be filed until all of the following requirements have been met:

- The four month time limit for presenting creditor claims has expired;
- All claims that were presented, expenses of administration, and taxes have been paid or otherwise dealt with;
- All property was distributed to the appropriate heirs;
- Arrangements have been made for unpaid claims, including notification of heirs of their continued liability for such claims;

- An accounting has been provided to the heirs, creditors, and other claimants whose claims are neither barred nor paid.

The personal representative should consider obtaining a receipt and waiver from the beneficiaries to reflect that each beneficiary (1) received a full accounting or waived the right to it, (2) has no further property rights to the estate, and (3) has no claim against the personal representative arising from the administration of the estate.

When does the appointment as personal representative end?

If the estate is closed informally with a closing statement, the appointment of personal representative will end officially one year after the closing statement is filed. *See ARS 14-3933(B).* Although nothing usually happens during this year, a personal representative does maintain the ongoing authority to sign a final tax return for the estate and deal with any miscellaneous matters that may arise.

If you were required to post a bond as personal representative, you may want to release the bond as soon as possible in order to curtail premium costs. Although technically you are still the personal representative for another year, the filing of a closing statement is generally adequate for a bonding company to release the bond. A prerequisite to filing of the closing statement is a final distribution of all the assets, so there is little or no risk to the bonding company.

Alternatively, an informal probate may be closed formally in order to obtain complete settlement of the estate without the one year waiting period. The formal closing requires a petition to be filed with the court requesting the court approve the final accounting, the distribution of the estate, and then discharge the personal representative from any further liability. *See ARS 14-3931.* The formal closing has strict notice requirements and will require a court hearing, but it has the benefit of bringing finality to the administration. The formal closing will terminate the proceeding.

The formal closing is generally preferred by estate attorneys when there are any disputes that have not been resolved or if the estate did not have enough assets to pay all claims fully. For the insolvent estate the formal closing will give notice to unpaid creditors and claimants so they can protect their future rights, if any.

Can I close the estate before filing the final tax return?

Yes. It is possible to file the closing statement in an informal probate without having filed the final income tax return. In order to do this you should consult with an accountant experienced with fiduciary returns so you can determine the potential tax liability. As personal representative you would accept the risk that the tax bill ends up being more than you have money set aside. Also, you may want to propose a prepayment of the accountant's fee for preparation of the final return.

If you feel comfortable doing so, as personal representative, you have a few options to set aside funds solely for payment of the final tax bill:

- Maintain adequate funds in a non-interest bearing account owned by the estate and disclose this fact on the final accounting and closing statement;
- Close the account but set aside funds in the IOLTA trust account of the estate attorney and disclose this fact on the final accounting and closing statement;
- Send payment of all remaining funds to the tax authorities and expect a small refund later. If the amount is nominal, it should not be difficult to cash the check at the bank where the estate account was kept. You may want to keep the account open temporarily with a zero balance.
- Transfer funds to a personal account and close the estate account. This may work fine if you are the only beneficiary.

TRUSTS

How does a trust settlement end?

A trust effectively terminates when it no longer owns any assets. If you are satisfied that all assets have been distributed, then you can proceed to close out your responsibilities.

Under ***ARS 14-10813(C)***, you must provide a final accounting to all of the current beneficiaries and any other beneficiaries who request it. The accounting must identify the receipts and disbursements, including the source and amount of trustee compensation. There is no form for the accounting. It is good practice to include copies of final statements showing a zero balance in financial accounts and copies of recorded transfer documents for real estate. The accounting need only have enough information to satisfy the curiosity of a reasonable beneficiary and to avoid controversy. A printed ledger from Quicken or Quick Books software may be sufficient. You might also suggest the possibility of having all the beneficiaries waive the right to an accounting. ***See ARS 14-10813(D).***

As trustee you are responsible for all tax reporting obligations. If necessary, you should file appropriate tax forms with the IRS and Arizona Department of Revenue to let them know that the trust has terminated and they should no longer anticipate any tax returns. An accountant can help you file these forms.

If the trust was administered properly, its termination will occur quietly and without any formal resolution.

Chapter 8

Special Topics

For some people the most important aspect of estate administration is the care of a pet. Arizona law even permits the use of pet trusts to ensure the long term care of cherished dogs and cats. This chapter discusses the care for surviving pets and other miscellaneous topics that deserve special attention.

What should I do with a surviving pet?

Articles and books about estate administration rarely discuss the topic of what to do with the deceased person's pets. But perhaps they should because it is very common to find a surviving pet alone in a deceased person's home. Usually the pet is a dog or cat, but sometimes the survivors might have to deal with fish, turtles, horses, hamsters, ferrets, or even snakes.

Finding a new home for a pet might be the first priority when administering an estate. After all, the pet may have been the deceased person's "best" friend.

The first step is to provide for the basic needs of the pet until the survivors can find a new home. That will mean giving proper care – making sure food is available and giving the pet a place to take care of business, in a matter of speaking.

The next step is to look carefully for any written instructions from the deceased person about who should inherit the pet. Absent any clear instructions, try contacting the animal's veterinarian. The phone number is likely on a refrigerator magnet or on the pet's collar. It is possible that the veterinarian recalls the pet and may know something important that you do not. The veterinarian may also have a kennel service to help care for the pet until a new home is found.

If you cannot find any instructions about who should inherit the pet, then you can ask around to see if anyone in the family – or possibly a close friend or neighbor – is interested in adopting the pet. This person could even be you. In some cases, you may not find anyone willing to take the pet. In other cases, the deceased owner may leave instructions to euthanize the animal because the owner believes the pet would never want to be with any other owner. Regardless, you should make every effort to honor the wishes of the pet's owner.

If euthanasia is chosen, one option is to retain a veterinarian to perform the service. Upon request and for an extra fee, you can probably find a veterinarian willing to travel to the home and handle it. A typical charge for this service is about $150. A second option is to contact the local humane society. The humane society will euthanize animals that are incurably ill, aged, or badly injured, and will seek alternatives for others. The cost is about $45 for this service, but it might require you to transport the animal – perhaps something easier said than done. The humane society even provides a cremation service, which is likely to cost approximately $50 to $100.

Some humane societies promise lifetime care for a pet in exchange for a monetary bequest from the owner's estate. For example, the Humane Society of Southern Arizona promotes its Guardian Angel program. This program is intended to deal with the high number of pets delivered to the humane society after the owner's death where the pet is still healthy. Even though the owner may have anticipated an adoption for the pet, it is likely that a new home will not be found. Thus, the Guardian Angel program provides the owner with assurance that the pet will be well cared for.

For a $2,500 minimum estate gift, the Humane Society of Southern Arizona will find a loving home for the pet. A gift of $10,000 or more will also include health insurance so you know that pet will get the care you expect. **www.hssaz.org**

May someone leave inheritance to a pet?

Yes. Arizona law permits pet owners to leave sums of money in trust for care of surviving pets. Under *ARS 14-2907* and *ARS 14-10408*, a pet owner may establish a trust for the life of a surviving pet. Although there is no limit to the amount of money you can put in the trust account, a court can reduce the amount if a judge feels it is excessive. The will or living trust should appoint a trustee and a successor, but a court can do it if necessary.

A trust may be established for multiple animals, and will end on the death of the last surviving animal. If there are funds left in the trust, the trust document should include a remainder beneficiary – usually a charitable organization.

How does the Medicare billing process work?

It is common for an estate administrator to collect a wide assortment of bills relating to the deceased person's last illness and hospital care. In many cases, the deceased person was enrolled in Medicare prior to death. There is no need to report the death to anyone at Medicare, but if you are unfamiliar with how Medicare works, the author does highly recommend obtaining a copy of the Medicare & You official handbook. This is an excellent resource covering the entire topic of Medicare. It can help you figure out how the billing system works. You can access the handbook through the Medicare website. **www.medicare.gov**.

Although enrollment in Medicare usually means there will be no major out-of-pocket expenses due, the personal representative should be prepared to pay the balance of the deceased person's annual deductible. In some cases, especially where the deceased person was fighting an illness for a long time, there may be medical bills that are not covered by Medicare or any other insurance. Thus, the personal representative may need to follow up with the insurance company to determine what amounts are actually owed.

The best approach is to notify the insurance company as soon as possible about the insured's death and inform the company who will be responsible for administering the estate. The insurance company will probably request a death certificate and proof that the person contacting them is responsible for the estate. If possible, direct the company to send all correspondence to the address of that person. Then continue to monitor all incoming "explanation of benefit" notices and bills that arrive. The EOB notices may be long and detailed. You should review them for charges that the patient (the deceased person) is responsible for. After a few months, or when medical bills appear to have stopped coming in, contact the insurance company to inquire about a final amount owed by the estate. If the amount is substantial, try negotiating a lower amount in exchange for prompt payment. It is not unreasonable (and in fact, not offensive to the company) to offer 50% to 75% of the invoiced amount. The insurance company will probably accept it. The beneficiaries might even complain to you if the invoiced amounts are paid in full.

The person responsible for administering the estate must be wary of proceeding too quickly. The worst case scenario occurs when a personal representative or trustee makes a full distribution to the beneficiaries before a major medical bill arrives. The personal representative or trustee is personally liable for a mistake of this nature. In a probate, the creditor notification requirements will reduce or eliminate any risk of this nature. But if you are administering the estate as trustee of a trust, or you plan to use small estate affidavits to administer the entire estate, then consider a proactive approach to creditor notification. As trustee, you could mail a notice to each known creditor and publish a notice to unknown creditors. *See ARS 14-6103(A)*. Alternatively, you may decide not to use small estate affidavits and instead use an informal probate action, which generally limits the time an unknown creditor may present a claim to four months after first publication. *See ARS 14-3803*.

How does a Medicare Advantage Plan work?

Medicare advantage plans provide wraparound coverage to persons who are entitled to Medicare Part A due to age, disability, or end-stage renal disease and have purchased Medicare Part B. The private insurer pays second. A well-known Medicare advantage plan is called TRICARE for Life. TRICARE is a benefit program for active and retired military personnel and their families, and TRICARE for Life is the product that provides wraparound Medicare coverage. For services covered by both Medicare and TRICARE for Life, the beneficiary pays nothing. For services covered by TRICARE for Life, but not Medicare, TRICARE is the primary payer. Costs and deductibles will vary depending on the plan. For services covered by Medicare, but not TRICARE for Life, the Medicare deductible and cost sharing applies. For services not covered by Medicare or TRICARE for Life, the beneficiary is responsible for the entire cost.

So what does this have to do with administering an estate? It is very common for an elderly person to tally up large unpaid medical bills prior to death. Since most elderly persons (over age 65) are enrolled in Medicare (and usually an advantage plan), the estate administrator is responsible for making sure all bills are handled properly. The estate administrator will need to review and understand the bills and the process for how they are paid. For those familiar with insurance billing practices, this will not be difficult. But it certainly is challenging for everyone else.

TRICARE for Life will request the sponsor's social security number when the estate administrator contacts them. The sponsor is the military service member who initially qualified for TRICARE coverage. Spouses and children are enrolled under the sponsor's identification. If unknown, gather as much information as possible about the sponsor before making the call.

How can I monitor or cancel the deceased person's Internet accounts?

A growing area of concern in estate administration is the handling of Internet accounts, also known as digital assets. Most people – including the elderly – now have multiple e-mail accounts and have memberships in social networking websites such as Facebook, Instagram, LinkedIn, Flickr, and YouTube.

If the deceased person was employed, contact the employer and suggest they forward e-mails to another employee for a while, and then close down the account.

It may take some considerable effort to access personal e-mail accounts. If you do not know the password, try looking around through important records and desk drawers for a list of passwords. If possible, try the password reset feature. At best you can use your knowledge of the deceased person's personal information to solve the password. At worst, the password was reset and no one will be able to access the account. For the accessible accounts, it is best to monitor each account for a while, and then make an effort to close them. For the others, it will probably be fine to just let them go. Eventually after a year or two, the account will close itself.

For personal websites, if possible, try printing out a copy of the website and then closing the account. If you cannot determine how the website is hosted, ask someone more familiar with website support and see if they can figure out who to contact about closing down the website. Although social networking websites such as Facebook may be an excellent tool to locate more extended relatives and acquaintances of the deceased person, the account should eventually be closed.

Facebook encourages the memorializing of an account after the death of a member. This involves a family member submitting an online form with proof of death (e.g., link to obituary) to Facebook. Memorializing the account removes certain sensitive information and sets privacy so that only confirmed friends can see the profile or locate it in search. The deceased person's wall remains active so that friends and family can leave posts in remembrance. Immediate family members may request the removal of an account. This will completely remove the account from Facebook so that no one can view it.

Many online or cloud-based services do not address the issue of death at all. However, Twitter permits a personal representative, with supporting legal documentation, to request an archive of the deceased person's public tweets and close the account.

What is an Inheritance Protection trust?

A fast growing area of estate planning involves "Inheritance Protection Trusts." If the deceased person retained an estate attorney recently to set up an estate plan, there is an excellent chance that inheritance was made payable to one or more of these trusts. Although the term "Inheritance Protection Trust" could generally describe many types of beneficiary trusts, it usually refers to a trust established for a responsible and healthy adult beneficiary. The trust is drafted to continue for the lifetime of the beneficiary, rather than end at a predetermined time or age of the beneficiary. The beneficiary often serves as sole trustee of the trust; thus, an Inheritance Protection Trust is commonly referred to as a "beneficiary-controlled trust."

By receiving inheritance in a trust, rather than receiving inheritance outright, the beneficiary can protect assets from various threats:

- *Estate tax protection.* If properly structured, the trust assets may be exempt from the federal estate tax upon the death of the beneficiary. When calculating the taxable estate of the deceased beneficiary, the trust assets would not be counted.

- *Creditor protection.* The trust assets are shielded from creditors of the beneficiary, even if insurance is insufficient to satisfy a judgment obtained by lawsuit. The trust can be drafted to provide enhanced levels of protection, if desired.

- *Divorce protection.* The trust assets are separate property of the beneficiary, and may not be converted to community property during marriage. This prevents an ex-spouse from penetrating the trust should the beneficiary's marriage end in divorce.

- *Family protection.* The trust may be drafted to insure that family assets pass to the next generation rather than to surviving spouses who may remarry. This protects the intent of the original owners, who may want the assets distributed to grandchildren.

The trust is used as an alternative to outright distribution when the amount of inheritance is expected to be substantial (generally more than $100,000). Its protective features are promoted as gifts to the beneficiary that cannot be obtained without formal estate planning. Typically the provisions of the trust are drafted into a will or living trust. The trust would not be funded with any assets until after the death of the original owner. In some cases the trust is established during the lifetime of the original owner, but this requires an irrevocable gift and usually loss of control over the gifted assets.

If the provisions of the trust are contained in a will or living trust, the personal representative or trustee – as the case may be – will be responsible for creating the trust during the weeks or months following the original owner's death. The process usually involves (1) formally appointing a trustee, (2) preparing a Certification of Trust, (3) applying for the Taxpayer ID number, and (4) opening an account in the name of the trust.

Why doesn't everyone use pay-on-death designations to avoid probate?

Pay-on-death designations and similar type beneficiary designations can be very helpful to avoid probate. In most cases they are simple to understand, implement, and carry out. So you may wonder why everyone does not use them for estate planning. To explain why, a summary of their disadvantages is presented here:

1. *Difficult to manage during owner's lifetime.* Many beneficiary designations are difficult to keep track of. When the owner wants to make a change to the overall plan, the owner must change the beneficiary for each bank account, insurance policy, investment account, property, etc. This is not an easy task, especially when compared to revising a will or living trust. Using beneficiary designations may actually require more effort by the owner than other "more complicated" approaches.

2. *Planning options are limited.* If an account owner intends to designate multiple beneficiaries using a pay-on-death designation, the beneficiaries can only inherit the account in equal, undivided shares. There is no option to allocate differently.

   A pay-on-death designation also does not consider the very real possibility that a beneficiary could predecease the owner. For example, assume Father named Son and Daughter as pay-on-death beneficiaries, but Daughter predeceased. Then the entire account would be distributed to Son and nothing would be distributed to Daughter's children, even though Father's intent may have been to include them.

   A pay-on-death designation fails to account for unusual situations. Payment to a minor or disabled child, for example, might trigger an unnecessary conservatorship or interfere with government benefits the child was entitled to.

   A pay-on-death designation also ignores a wide range of trust planning techniques to protect a beneficiary's inheritance in the event of lawsuit, divorce, or poor investment management.

3. *Ignores Incapacity Planning.* A pay-on-death designation is disregarded during the owner's lifetime, and makes no effort to plan for the owner's possible incapacity. The owner will usually rely on a durable power of attorney, although they are notoriously unreliable.

Why do estate attorneys rarely suggest joint ownership of an asset between parent and child?

Many elderly persons add a child as joint owner of cash accounts and real property during their lifetime. Estate attorneys rarely recommend this strategy for several reasons:

1. *Exposes parent's assets to the child's creditors.* If the child is sued, the child must disclose the joint asset to the court. The burden falls on the child to convince a court that the child contributed nothing and that the asset really belongs to the parent. Similarly, the account would be a reportable asset if the child filed for bankruptcy protection.

2. *Child gets divorced.* If the child gets divorced, the ex-spouse may argue that all or a portion of the joint asset is really owned by the child and it becomes part of the settlement negotiations.

3. *Child needs money.* When a child is joint owner, there is nothing to prevent the child from withdrawing some or all of the funds or using the asset as collateral to get a loan. This could happen without the parent's knowledge or consent.

4. *Parent and Child disagree about management of asset.* The parent loses full control of the asset – especially real estate – because the child would have to sign off on a sale, refinance, or reverse mortgage. This might be seen as a good thing when everyone gets along, but even the best relationships can fall apart.

5. *Assumes Child is a saint.* The parent can only hope the child "does the right thing" and uses the joint asset to pay estate bills and then shares it equally among all the children. The child's estate attorney would be correct under the law to counsel the child otherwise.

6. *Possible loss of property tax breaks.* The parent may lose eligibility for low income property tax breaks if the home is owned jointly by another person.

7. *Possible loss of homestead exemption.* The parent may jeopardize the homestead exemption, which provides creditor

protection, by conveying an interest in the home to another person. *See ARS 33-1104.*

8. *No full step-up in basis.* Most property benefits from a full step-up in income tax basis at the death of its owner. If the property is owned as joint tenants with right of survivorship, the property only receives a one-half step-up in basis at the parent's death. For example, if Dad paid $200,000 for the property and it was worth $400,000 at Dad's death, then tax laws permits a step-up in basis to $400,000. Then the child could sell the property right away with no capital gains tax. On the other hand, if the property was jointly owned with the child, the basis would increase by only one-half, to $300,000, and there could be an extra $100,000 of taxable gain upon sale.

9. *Potential eligibility penalties upon application for ALTCS nursing home benefits.* The parent must report gifts made within the prior five years when applying for nursing home benefits through the ALTCS program. The value of the gift may trigger a penalty and delay the start of benefits.

Epilogue

How to Make Sure your Estate Plan Actually Works

Y ou may wonder about the adequacy of your own estate plan while reading this book. Whether you have retained an estate attorney to help you or not, here are some suggestions you can follow to make sure your estate plan really works the way you intended it.

Talk about your Estate Plan with Family

The best way to minimize disappointment and arguments after your death is to let everyone know what to expect in advance. You should be prepared to discuss the general structure of your estate plan with your family. You might even want to make changes to your estate plan based on these conversations. Of course, you are not required to share copies of documents with anyone, but there are good reasons to share why you made certain decisions when you are still able to explain them.

The author recalls a client who carefully prepared her advance medical directives. She told the son she named as her agent what she wanted, and she completed all the documents correctly. When she fell ill, her daughter (who had not maintained much contact) could not believe her mother would want to refuse medical care. The daughter initiated legal proceedings to force continued aggressive treatment. She was unsuccessful, but the cost and heartache were both considerable – and brother and sister no longer speak to one another. Mom could have avoided that outcome – perhaps – if she had discussed her wishes with both children.

Don't Tinker with Asset Titling or Beneficiary Designations

Refrain from making changes to your estate plan without prior review and counsel from your estate attorney. For example, if someone at your bank or credit union suggests you convert all your accounts into pay-on-death accounts, please talk to your estate attorney first. If your banker tells you that your attorney "just doesn't know how banks work," remind him that he is not a legal expert on this topic. Likewise, if your estate attorney has helped you name a trust as beneficiary of your IRA and your accountant tells you that is a mistake, please talk to your estate attorney before you change it back.

Please do not add a child's name to the deed for your house, or your bank account, "just in case." Your estate plan should already take care of "just in case," and your changes may undo the value and effect of the documents prepared for you.

Coordinate your Beneficiary Designations

If your will leaves everything to your children equally, but your life insurance policy designates only your oldest daughter as beneficiary, then your daughter gets the proceeds after your death. The equal provision in your will is disregarded. Is that what you intend? If so, make it clear. If not, change the beneficiary designation to match your will. Different considerations are involved with life insurance, IRAs, and other kinds of policies; ask your estate attorney for assistance in getting your beneficiary designations arranged. They are often more important than your will or living trust.

Prepare a Personal Property Memorandum

Your estate plan probably includes a provision that permits you to designate individual items of personal property (e.g., jewelry, antiques, collections, cars) to specific persons. Complete that list, even if it remains a work in progress. The list does not need to mention every item in your house, but it should identify beneficiaries for items of special interest or value. The author has regularly observed how family and friends enjoy discovering that they were remembered on such a list. Following through with this task conveys a special message to your beneficiaries.

Prepare a List of Assets and Directions

The person responsible for settling your estate will greatly appreciate any list of account numbers, debts, and similar financial information that you might leave behind. You may know exactly where the life insurance policy is that you bought in 1985 or how often the statement from your little credit union in Wisconsin arrives. But your survivors may not, and the person responsible for settling your estate may spend countless hours looking for that kind of information. In addition, you can substantially alleviate your family's stress immediately upon your death if you leave some direction about the funeral arrangements you desire and the information necessary to acquire a death certificate.

Determine Whether your Durable Financial Power of Attorney Will Work

It is good practice to submit a copy of your financial power of attorney to your financial institutions, especially if you are elderly or in poor health. Many financial institutions will routinely reject a perfectly-valid power of attorney simply because it is not the financial institution's proprietary form. By submitting a copy of your attorney-drafted power of attorney, you may discover that your financial institution has this silly rule. But, at least, then you will have an opportunity to sign its proprietary form and avoid this problem.

Addendum

Sample Trust Beneficiary Notification
Under ARS §14-10813

Beneficiary:
Michael Williams
999 S. Central Ave.
Tucson, AZ 85700
(520) 555-1111

Decedent/Trustor:
Susan Williams
Date of death-   June 1, 2013
Place of death- Pima County, Arizona

Trust Name:
Susan Williams Living Trust dated June 1, 2011

Trustee:
Matthew Williams
111 N. Main St.
Tucson, AZ 85799
(520) 555-2222

Notice:
You have received this notification because you are a current beneficiary of the trust named above. Although you have not yet received any distributions from the trust, Arizona trust law gives you specific rights to information about the trust. You may wish to consult with an attorney to review your rights under the Arizona Trust Code.

Copy of Trust:
Under ARS §14-10813(B)(1), the trustee is required to send you, upon request, a copy of the portions of the trust document that are necessary to describe your interest.

Trustee Reports:

Under ARS §14-10813(C), the trustee is required to send you a trustee's report, at least annually, and at the termination of the trust, of the trust assets and liabilities accompanied by a ledger showing all receipts and disbursements during the prior reporting period, including the source and amount of the trustee's compensation.

Status Updates:

Trust settlement is a complex and time-consuming process. The trustee requests your patience and understanding. However, if you need information about the status of the trust settlement, please contact the trustee or the trustee's attorney: Thomas J. Bouman, 7650 E. Broadway Blvd. #108, Tucson, AZ 85710, (520) 546-3558, tom@tomboumanlaw.com.

To inquire about legal counsel specific
to your situation, please contact:

Bouman Law Firm

7650 E. Broadway Blvd. #108

Tucson, AZ 85710

(520) 546-3558

www.TomBoumanLaw.com

Also:

www.wealthcounsel.com

www.avvo.com

www.azbar.org

www.naela.org

www.specialneedsalliance.org